ERIC OWEN MOSS

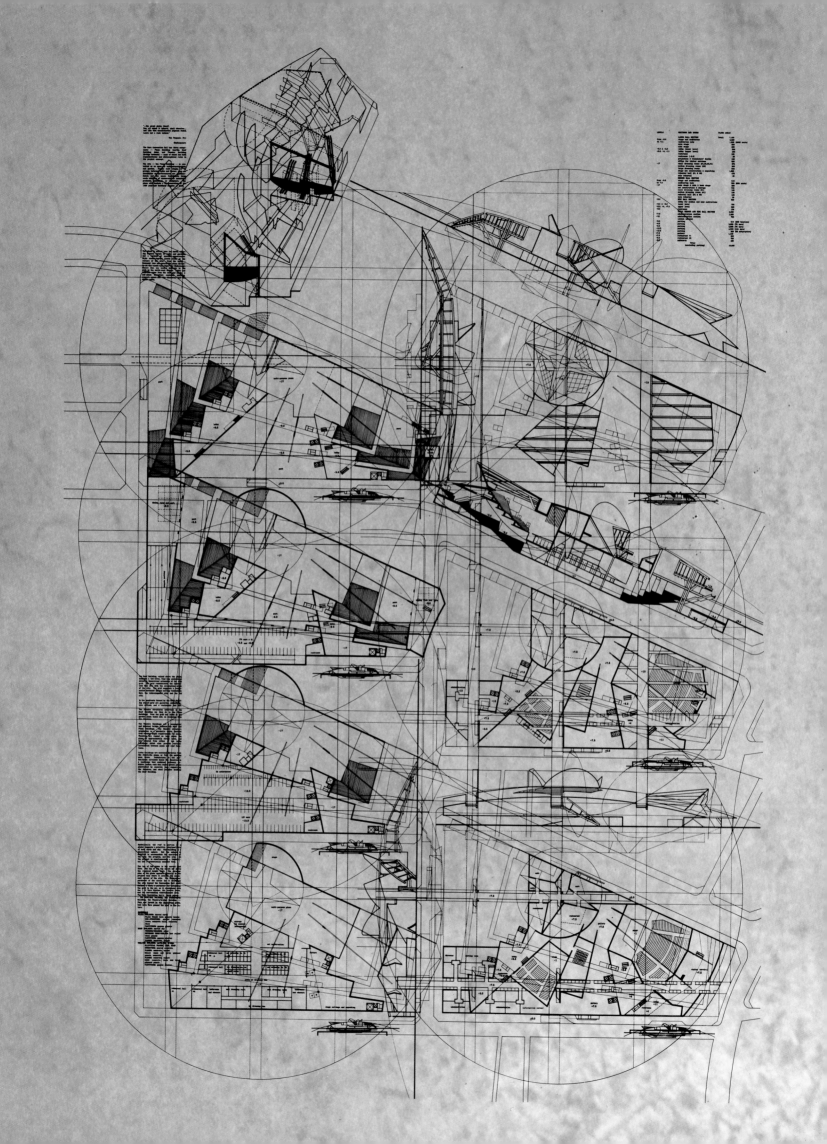

Architectural Monographs No 29

ERIC OWEN MOSS

A.D. ACADEMY EDITIONS • EN ERNST & SOHN

To Ruth

Never to keep, really; never the same for the clock-
    shaped, corpse-caped schemer to ports.
There – theirs – never.

Sennetts from the Tortuguise
Moss Herbert

Architectural Monographs No 29
Editorial Offices
42 Leinster Gardens London W2 3AN

Editor: James Steele
Editorial and Design Team: Andrea Bettella (Senior Designer),
Gina Williamson (Design); Nicola Hodges, Natasha Robertson (Editorial)

Acknowledgements
Special thanks to: James Steele, Mary Eaves Mitchell,
Jay Vanos, Scott M Nakao, Todd Conversano, Dennis Ige

Office Staff of Eric Owen Moss Architects: Jay Vanos, Scott M Nakao, Todd
Conversano, Dennis Ige, Thomas Ahn, Andreas Aug, Annette Baghdasarian,
Greg Baker, Marco Benjamin, Ann Bergren, Loren Beswick, Alan Binn, Amedee
Butt, Teng-chin Chen, Su-shien Cho, Alfred Chow, Domingo Cuevas, Isabel
Duvivier, Mary Eaves Mitchell, Inaki Erostarbe, Jorge V Suso Fernandez-
Figares, Augis Gedgaudas, Diane Gourdal, Paul Groh, Mark Harris, Sophie
Harvey, Eric D Holmquist, Carol Hove, Gevik Hovsepian, Scott B Hunter,
Sheng-yuan Hwang, Amanda Hyde, Mathias Johannsen, Lisa Kim, Andreas
Kirberg, Christine Lawson, Anderson Lee, Mark Lehman, Jae Lim, Christoph
Lueder, Paris Mamikunian, Dana Mansfield, Maureen McGuire Moss, Mogens
Milbach, Karin Mahle, Ana Paula Moi, Lawrence O'Toole, Urs Padrun, Jose
Pimentel, Sumathi Ponnambalam, Jennifer Rakow, Andy Ratzsch, Eric Rich,
Lucas Rios, Eduoardo Sabater, Elissa Scrafano, Nick Seierup, Naoto Sekiguchi,
Daryusch Sepehr, Elisabeth Springefeldt Goncalves de sa Peixoto, Eric Allen
Stultz, Ravindran Kodalur Subramanian, Jerry Sullivan, Dana Swinsky Cantelmo,
Janek Tabencki Dombrowa, Evelyn Tickle

Cover: Aronoff; *Page 2:* Nara Convention Center, Japan

First published in Great Britain in 1993 by
ACADEMY EDITIONS
An imprint of the Academy Group Ltd

ACADEMY GROUP LTD
42 Leinster Gardens London W2 3AN
ERNST & SOHN
Hohenzollerndamm 170, 1000 Berlin 31
Members of VCH Publishing Group

ISBN 1 85490 189 3 (HB)
ISBN 1 85490 190 7 (PB)

Distributed to the trade in the United States of America by
ST MARTIN'S PRESS
175 Fifth Avenue, New York, NY 10010

Printed and bound in Singapore

CONTENTS

FOREWORD

The
city emboldens its builder,
a man can hide in the city,
a man can swathe himself in the city;
wrap the city around his shoulders like a shawl,
impupil the city in his eyes,
consume the city through his ears,
drug his nostrils with the city,
daily go forth encinctured by the quartz fabric
    of the city,
quaff the city, tousle the city upon his pillow,
copulate according to the canons of the city's beat,
flake off a body in the city as if the actual
    were the city,
assume these bastions, turrets and pavements as
    biologic as trees.
A man is more in the city –
the clanging city of erection
where clad power throbs
through penes of steep stone;
the city is his potency –
this fragile tick,
this thin bleat contemptuous of thunders the
    city walls out
until suddenly it ceases in the city.
Hurry – rush it from the city,
shunt it underground.
That is all. What else can be done?
Forget, forget,
we must save ourselves,
do you wish to destroy the city?
do you wish to expose us in our nakedness to the
    terrors without?
Hush, hush,
forget,
go your way about the city,
suck avidly the newspapers of the city,
wallow in the roaring radio of the city,
devise a duty in the city,
suffer for want of what the city holds prize,
exult on seizing the spoil of the city,
fasten your self like a fungus on the city,
prattle of the future in the city's glib speech,
cut posture to the matrix of the city,
enform the flesh –
these are graved high on the tablets of the city.
What prowess a man has in the city,
and see how soon, untallied, he dissolves amid
    the droves.
How impregnable, that – untallied,
how fortunate for the ramparts of the city,
how dreadful if it were otherwise,
how dreadful for the city.
                                            Hatch
out your projects in the city,
dream designs far-leaping
from the fleshwarm verticals of the city
where voluminous distance lurks entrapped,
unrecognised, unfeared,
and the incessant surf of silence breaks unheard
except in queer-sick instants quickly spent.

Hurl from the mother stronghold of the city
harpoons to thrall the infinite and immeasurable,
reduce gigantic earth to vanquishment –
its brute mountains, proliferating forests,
blurring sands and stout, unspooling plains,
its tensioned seas unplumbed
sloshing in toothtorn hollows;
with desperate art,
strung wires poled and cunning bands of road,
bind landscape, dumb, enormous,
captive to the city;
the skies,
hanging illimitable with menace
over the phallic city,
transform to gelded constellations
acknowledging the city's yoke.
                                            Heroic
hoodwinker,
furious artificer of masks for perpetual
    All-Fool's Day,
mountebank weaver of peacock-hued snares,
    traps, veils and pitfalls;
mystifier of genius,
indefatigable tactician fecund with impostures
    of gag and blinkers
textured of ostentation, stateliness and belled
    solemnities
to reassure the master of his masteries
in spite of whisper.
                                            O
the raw land without end
and sky without end
and man, fallen outsprawled on the land, the
    raw, pitiless, endless land,
sight thrust beseechingly into the bitter
    endlessness above –
only the man had end
and he trembled,
for how could he breathe knowing all this
    endlessness?
How could he fashion here his home?
How could he walk not an alien here?
How could he find warmth here and compassion
on the smooth land, the jagged land, the barren
    land, the upswirling, precipiced land
waiting with interminable patience under
    chameleon endlessness of sky,
which, too, with monumental patience waited?
So, fear furiated,
the megalomaniac city,
the city of supreme delusion,
the unspeakable city
booming and crashing
in terrible, uptowering waves of impact
reverberated from a huge gong
tubercular with sound of ruse triumphant.

From 'Who's Lyric', by Moss Herbert

7

8522 National Boulevard Complex,
Hybrid Arts

Eric Owen Moss: I need an epigram that gives a sense of what drives the work. I don't want to sound like I'm walking around with the Unabridged Webster trying to be the most esoteric person on earth. I don't want that, but I don't want to denigrate an intellectual instinct either. You don't know where to go sometimes. It's not Either/Or; it's Neither/Nor. You're looking for a map. And you can't use someone else's.

James Steele: You're trying to find perspective.

EOM: I think what I want is for architecture to deal with this personal map making because it's the only subject. Everything else comes after. Maybe it could have been something else for me besides architecture – writing, or drawing, or something destructive. Like Roskolnikov hitting the old lady with an axe . . .

JS: Is that what it's about for you then?

EOM: Architecture as an axe (and maybe a stiletto too). Yesterday I was talking to a young student from Vienna and I wanted to say something that would horrify her. I wanted to test her limits, see how resilient she was. I'm not sure why. I started talking about a chapter in *The Possessed*. Things stick in your head and other things run out. What sticks? So this story stuck. Stavrogin raped a seven-year old girl. This was his confession. The destructive side. Years ago Karen Stein came to a lecture in New York and said something like, 'OK, I've seen the work and I wanted to hear the rap'. Everybody has his rap. It's all promotional. So it's not all promotional. You get desperate sometimes when you're sitting here by yourself. And then somebody comes to you and says this is a hype.

JS: How much of that destructiveness, or nihilism do you think is a factor of location, of Los Angeles?

EOM: None.

JS: None?

EOM: None.

JS: Can you say that . . .

EOM: Categorically?

JS: Categorically!

EOM: It's the old problem. Nothing to do with local physiology. I mean old old. Canetti said the most influential book he had ever read was *Gilgamesh*.

The story goes back about 4,000 years. They dug it up about 100 years ago. Doesn't matter where Gilgamesh lived.

I like thinking you know where you're going and suddenly something jerks you in another way. You're suspicious about where you were going originally, so

you move. Gilgamesh shifted my direction. This is apropos of your question about whether LA made me do it. Gilgamesh made me do it. The British are always saying it's LA, it's LA. This is wrong. It's not whether it rains here, or whether there is no city to the city. That's a different discussion. But underneath everything I think what drives my work (aside from the usual ambition and vanity) is the Gilgamesh problem.

JS: Of searching.

EOM: Gilgamesh is the King and his buddy is a sort of 'natural man' raised by the wolves named Enkidu. They fight a monster. Enkidu gets killed. Gilgamesh can't accept death and loss and time and history and what's finite and all of that so he goes on a journey, trying to find the secret. He crosses the lake of death in a row boat. The oars get eaten, but not the boat, so consistency wasn't a virtue here either. Gilgamesh finds the one who knows the secret. The guy gives him a flower. Gilgamesh goes back. He's sitting on a beach, goes for a swim, and while he's swimming (it's always a serpent) the serpent comes up and eats the flower. Eats the secret.

JS: So you were really involved in a deeper sense with the ideas of good and evil.

EOM: Nothing is very neat. The problems of living are overlapping. Vanity, and competition, and BS are mixed with Gilgamesh.

We were doing a show in New York. Some lady came up to me and said, boy, there are a lot of important people here. And so I started to laugh and I told her take a walk through the local graveyard, come back and tell me if she still felt the same way. Sounds a little Talmudic, huh?

JS: Yes.

EOM: She understood, I think, so she immediately went away and had a drink and recovered.

JS: What's the epigram?

EOM: It's from something which you would very much love called *The Writer's Profession* by Canetti. I'll read it to you. 'He's closest to the world when he carries a chaos inside himself yet he feels responsibility for this chaos. He does not approve of it . . .' (so this is not a chaos promotion). 'He does not feel at ease about it, he does not regard himself as grand for having room for so many contradictory and unconnected things. He hates the chaos, he never gives up hope of overcoming it for others and thereby for himself as well. To utter anything of any value about this world, he cannot push it away and avoid it.'

I'm afraid of posturing. I don't want to give that impression, but on the other hand, I don't want to

9

8522 National Boulevard Complex, Goalen Group

shrink from dealing with questions that are of interest to me. There's another epigram to one of my Dad's books, also from Canetti: Here it is, 'One shall seek nothingness only to find a way out of it, and one shall mark the road for everyone.' This is pretty good. It doesn't say how, doesn't say who, and if you're the who, the one who has that job, you don't really have any choice. I have no choice except the choice to uncover what my choice really is. In retrospect no choice. So architecture is a moral imperative for me. Leave a sign to the next guy, a sign on the road from nothingness. The act of doing architecture, the primordial act, contests nothingness.

JS: Some choices are closed.

EOM: I think the objective is to be what you are. This doesn't mean you know yourself. I think what you want is to be yourself.

JS: How did this all start, this love of geometry, this instinct for form?

EOM: I would call it an emotive geometry. This instinct is coming to an end for me. It's still strong in the Westen House. In projects like Nara, and the Westen House there are a series of governing geometries, plural. What I've done is pull them together. So they infect each other. Make a hybrid. But the first premiss, a recognisable geometry, precedes the project. Pre-exists. The premiss is durable. It belongs to the history of building, of setting limits, of measure. It's conservative. And it's inadequate, doesn't say what I want it to say. I'm acknowledging some continuity. But also the need to move, or to alter, or to find a way to build that is original and personal. How to jump over myself and everybody else? There are arguments about whether these qualities can be built into architecture. I guess I'll find out.

Geometry gave me a reference, a history, a way to use what pre-existed, and then to abuse it and to alter it so that I could make something which was known and unknown, both. When I make something which is known, I also make something which I don't know. As things close down, others open up. No permanent solutions. As you're resolving things, you're unravelling things. Makes me feel dangerous. I used to tease Linda, the lady who owns the Westen House, about what I call the Penelope theory of architecture.

Penelope put the quilt together during the day and then took it apart at night. A great metaphor for building . . . making something and dismantling it simultaneously. Now there's an ulterior motive in Penelope's case, which is to stall until Odysseus shows up. You're putting something together and you're procrastinating and you build this conceptual procrastination right into the project.

JS: So nothing is even finished for you, but is a continuity.

EOM: You're making something and then contesting its validity. This is not like saying I have no sense of where the project is going. It doesn't mean

everything's possible. Maybe it means everything's a possible beginning. The priority is the building.

I'm not saying this makes me mysterious, and esoteric, and unabridged Webster-ish. I'm just saying this is the only way available because there isn't anything else outside me that doesn't collapse when I push. You don't get at the truth by insisting. This isn't a synonym for architectural nihilism. It means architecture sneaks up from contrary directions.

JS: An element of subversiveness is also there.

EOM: But I don't mean to sound like a Berkeley subversive. That was adolescent. I think I got over that, although I get a certain amount of energy out of contesting the world, as if it were purposeful and homogeneous. Attacking the banks? The clients? The mayor of Vienna? Whoever is diabolical that week? But these are all external, extroverted. A deeper architecture starts with the introverted.

JS: You work through these themes, I mean I've seen the geometry, the themes, the ravelling and unravelling.

EOM: Right.

JS: You work through ideas, don't you?

EOM: In the Westen House, one could conceivably reconstitute the geometry using the constituent components of the house and return to several recognisable pieces. Pieces of the pieces are removed in the house. So some parts are literal some theoretical. You don't get the geometric totality immediately, but it's available by implication. It can be worked on intellectually. But experientially, the space has no total. So why imply resolution? Completeness? The Stealth project, is an evolving form. Like Heraclitus' river. You never step into the same form twice. The effort is to avoid the static. No resolution. But articulate irresolution. The Stealth starts as three sided and becomes four sided. No warped surfaces. Only flat planes. Moves from three to four over its 100 metre length. Stop it at any point in section, and you see perpetual transformation. The Squid and the conference room in the Hayden Tower project use similar devices, the Squid in section, the conference room in plan. No more potential for intellectual resolution or completion.

JS: OK. So you're not seeking resolution, you're looking for changes.

EOM: I came to the end of that in Westen. Another example. About six years ago I got interested in the ellipse. It has an order: you can write its equation. It has one centre, it has two centres, it has three centres. The 8522 National conference room is a conical ellipse. But you can't have a conical ellipse because a cone resolves itself at one point and the ellipse equation has two centres. But the top of the ellipse is sawed off. So the two centres don't have to become one. The ellipse is adjusted but not demolished. The identity, the power of the form, holds. And

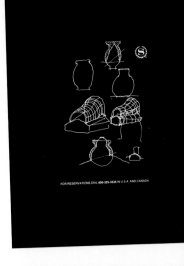

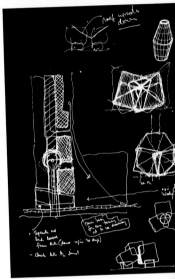

it's retraceable to a recognisable whole. And a hole. Both. Whole or hole? The Gilgamesh problem again: you want it to start with a *w* but a lot of times it's an *h*.

JS: A black hole.

EOM: Yes.

JS: Does the black hole have any bearing on the way you detail?

EOM: The antecedents for this discussion are Marcel Lods and John Prouve. LA gets a lot of credit for its tactile sensibilities. There are earlier, braver people who ought to get the credit. The 'off the shelf', the industrial, the pre-fabricated – the image – the romanticised industry of the teens and 20s. Fighting an aristocracy (McKim, or Versailles) Fighting an old tradition made a new tradition. Time to kick down that one too. Le Corbusier writes *In Defence of Architecture* and dedicates it to Alexander Vesnin. These guys are pals, with a common enemy. I like those personal connections. Architectural and personal. They help.

JS: Can you be more specific?

EOM: Ziva Freiman was making a book, *Shoulder to Shoulder, Back to Back.* Himmelblau, Mayne, Holl, Woods, Sorkin, Moss at the barricades. Sounds terrifying.

JS: Yes, it does!

EOM: The material question – what's used and why – is about an aesthetic predilection. And predilection is weakness. It's derived, doesn't belong to me. So I'm trying to unlearn it. The selection of materials has become easy which means it's not a choice anymore. It's been made for you. The buildings I've done (aside from throwing around some granite in the Westen House) are expensive because of their labour costs. To pay for it you find some cheap acrylic, some two-bit Z's. In order to make the form, the object, you find some cheap material, so you can afford the labour. The order of the form and the space are the experience. Form and space have to be made out of something. So how can I get this built? The visual aspirations of the cheap material palette were set by European predecessors who had a different agenda. So the current preferences are disingenuous. I'm not saying the argument hasn't moved. The off-the-shelf business has been altered here because in making things that are odd, or idiosyncratic, or personal, you wind up making them with love, with great care. So the pre-fabricated, make a billion of them argument supplied the conceptual materials for making the single, crafted, idiosyncratic object.

Everything big is made from things small. You put the small together with finesse. The assembly line admonition is irrelevant. The 8522 conference table is made out of doors. If you don't point out the doors, people don't notice. They're surprised, and this alludes to a general operational principle in my work: I'm not sure of the conventional identity of a

door, a window, a wall, a roof, a column. What are they? I have no dictionary. The Prince of Wales has a dictionary. The people that built Seaside have a dictionary. So a door could surreptitiously become a table.

JS: I have also noticed that in detailing, you usually expose the surface, you get a sensibility edge in there, you don't bury the edge.

EOM: That's not an ideological decision. The ideology ought to be that there's no ideology, and in fact I can see what people are talking about when they say these images are contagious. Images can be taught, learned, repeated until they're lifeless. Everyone looks for the rule. In this case, it's the detailing rule. But it's no esta. Find your own way, and not somebody else's. This is work which in principle would like to say there are no allegiances. So this is Trotsky's theory of permanent revolution. Never works politically. But it can work personally. If you could actually live like this, formulating and re-formulating. Where's the durable formula?

The Stealth project, and the Aronoff project are trying to see in a new way. They contradict the value of my experience. You're older but you still don't know. You're different. You have the same name.

There's a slide of a construction excavation in Mexico City: Aztec Tenochitlan, replaced by the Spanish Mexico City, replaced by the contemporary circumstance. One civilisation piling its truth on the previous truth. Which is no longer there. Tenochitlan – gone. Cortez – gone. The original title of the Rizzoli article was 'Which lie do you want to tell?'. I had another slide of Chichinitza where they built one layer on top of the other, with grass growing over the entire thing. As if the buildings never happened. Another slide was a 4,000 year old Babylonian map of the sky.

JS: You refer to that quite a bit, it is obviously important to you. Why?

EOM: Why do you draw a map of the sky? I can tell you why. Because psychologically the sense of earth alone is impossible. Can you imagine some guy walking around with a rhino after him, three sabre-toothed tigers, dinosaurs, and here comes Noah. So you have to predict: know the past; know the future. We know where to go. We're safe. Cities are like this. Cities measure, divide, align, order. A psychic necessity. Try living without it.

JS: It has always been the basis for architecture.

EOM: You want to find a way to say that measure counts, that life has a scale. I have a slide of a scale which is bent. It's funny when you talk about geometry which is related to order, and to equations. I mean you have to go somewhere, which suggests a way to continue to go ahead, so the Babylonians did. They made a map and it's wrong. Left out a few things. We have maps, and they're wrong also. But I think the presumption of technology and science was that the discovery of truth was asymptotic to the movement of time. So as time passed, we would

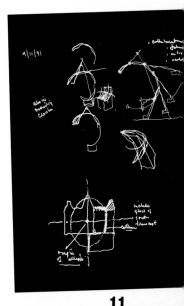

11

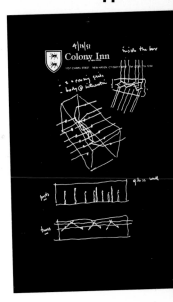

know more and more and finally we would get there. False. We're never going to get there, and I think the thing about Penelope which is so profound is that as you learn things you get rid of things. So in some ways Babylon knew what we can't, and knowing or thinking you know, (which is a better way to put it) in certain areas seems to rule out knowing other areas. So you never get there, you never get there. But you keep trying. There's something in you that pushes. I've often wondered where it comes from.

JS: Why do you keep trying?

EOM: Yeah, it's funny, I was giving this lecture in Toronto the other night, so afterwards, a local newspaper critic, a raucous sort of character, was laughing and she said she was walking out with somebody who said, 'you know, he's crazy'. PERIOD. I'm not crazy. I'm starting to think that I can understand why I don't understand, so if I can't always say I know what to do, I think I can say what I won't do. We're going to get some opportunities now to see where all of this goes architecturally, and I think that what I'm saying can be built very poignantly. In other words, you can regurgitate your pain architecturally. This is not grandiose, OK? This is what the man said: 'He never gives up hope of overcoming it for others, and thereby himself and he does not regard himself as grand for having room for so many contradictory things.' A moral imperative for architecture.

EOM: In *Ecclesiastes* it's one generation goeth, another cometh. And I try to jump over that. I'm trying to get on top of it, see it another way, understand it, attack it, open it up. Pascal, the mathematician, was also a philosopher. He used the metaphor that life was a march to the guillotine, and the only way you could alter the pattern was to jump out of line, run up to the front, and stick your head under the blade. He said that. Pascal.

I want to rupture it, or get on top of it. I'm always trying to wrap my arms around it and say OK I got it now. Wright, Le Corbusier, Kahn – they all want to tell us the way it is. This is the way it is. It's like this. But it's not like this. I would like to make a premiss out of the idea of the evolving premiss. You come to the truth momentarily. Then you lose it again.

Nara is geometric and ageometric. Originates in a globe. In the description I used Prospero's line: '. . . the great globe itself, yea all which it inherit, shall dissolve and . . . leave not a rack behind. We are such stuff as dreams are made on, and our little life is rounded with a sleep.' Very beautiful. The project is about the dissolution of the globe. Nara is actually at the end of the Chinese silk road, an early grid. Not quite Hippodamus and Miletus, but a very old grided city. The grid system amends the ball and the ball amends the grid.

There's a second symbolism in Nara learned from the Caracol, the only round building in Chichinitza. It's a different sensibility, a non-Western sensibility. There's some inclination to say that the West shouldn't define everything, doesn't know everything. That seems obvious. The problem is that often the people who are arguing against the West are simply uncritical promoters of other groups. You don't study Shakespeare to promote the West. With Nara there's the carved earth and there's the sky, which is the lid of the ball. And there are theatres on legs, which bridge between earth and sky. An old way of seeing and understanding. But now it's private and personal, not societal. We're the first generation to which the cross fertilisation of cultures, ecumenical cultures, is entirely available. How can you pick the Pantheon after visiting the Caracol? You have to use both. Or neither. The Yucatan is a ferocious sensibility. They want to yank your heart out. I was interested in bringing that quality to Nara. I don't think I was able to do that. It's too intellectual and too cerebral, and too analytical, and I don't know if it's possible to transfer that kind of mystery across time.

JS: Aronoff has the same geometry.

EOM: In the Aronoff house, the geometry has a different aspiration. That house sits on the edge of a hill, looking down into a forest. It began as a ball on the edge of a hill. There it goes . . . I don't know whether this is legible in the project but it should suggest instability, disequilibrium. Is it going to roll away, or is it going to stay? In the end the decision (not only for insurance company reasons) is that it decides on the side of stability, but barely. And it's made out of stones. Orthogonal stones. Hard to roll an orthogonal stone.

JS: The brick association of the United States should love it.

EOM: It's block actually. They're going to give us the block as a promotion. It's a tapered block, tapered in plan and tapered in section . . .

JS: To deal with the rains . . .

EOM: To deal with the curve in two directions. But the block face remains straight. The house has a spherical order. You acknowledge it, then you reverse it. The block components are orthogonal. So is it square? Round? The house has both aspects but is never entirely either. So it always is and isn't. Either or and neither nor.

JS: I know you're going to hate it if I mention Jacques Derrida.

EOM: I won't.

EOM: I got interested in the writing of Paul Deman, Derrida's mentor, who was an English professor at Yale for many years. When architecture wants to give itself an intellectual hypodermic it finds something profound. Deconstructivism is an example, but Deman is important. So is Derrida. Their work is about understanding and its constituent parts. Architecture can actually possess and absorb everything. It's always bigger than what you say it is. The content of Deconstruction was there before it was labelled. Diverse meanings, multiple meanings, no meaning, and the measure of meaning.

TS Eliot wrote about the 'still point of the turning world'. I remember Bobby Kennedy paraphrasing a Bernard Shaw remark about the truth as a circuitous trickle working its way between two banks of a river. So Bobby Kennedy and TS Eliot are Deconstructivists. The label hurts more than it helps. As soon as you use it, you're obliged to define it.

Deconstruction is an affirmation of a stage of not knowing. That's positive. What Canetti was saying was, don't be satisfied with the not knowing. The idea is to get out of it, not to promote wallowing. There's more to that Canetti quote: 'whether in grief or in despair, one shall endure in order to learn how to save others from it. But not out of scorn for the happiness that the creatures deserve even though they deface one another and tear one another to pieces.'

So Thomas Hobbes was a Deconstructivist. I think the Deconstructivist discussion is useful. It's not a question of whether you like it or not; it's necessary. You have to go through it.

I had a student at Yale who went to the Music Library, and made xerox's of John Cage's scores. Do you know the scores?

JS: Yes I do.

EOM: They're very beautiful. Then of course the student tried to make architecture out of that. There was one sound running along the staff, continuously rising and falling, an almost cosine curve. Then Cage draws a straight line that touches the cosine notes at a number of points. So the curve notes are intersected by the straight line note. Visual music.

There's another very interesting composer named Boulez. His music abrogates the conventional author's responsibility. Boulez writes ten sections and tells you to provide the chronology, the sequence. So he's telling us there's no single sequence. Sequence becomes plural. You can't rearrange the notes, but what you can do is set up the order. It limits the authority of the composer. Aesthetic egalitarianism. I'm opposed, but I'm sympathetic.

Cage had another compositional game. He used a clear acrylic staff. He placed notes on the page, all over the page. Then the player moved the acrylic staff up and down the page. Where it stops he plays the notes, as written, so the notes belong to both the composer and the player. Taking personal possession of the art. Obligate the players, and by implication the audience. I think this is part of the discussion of Deconstruction. Who hears what you hear?

JS: So it's denying the role of the author.

EOM: It obviates the role of the author. I think it contests the single-mindedness of the work. No single mind. Maybe it's also a generous instinct. It has to do with sharing, or we're all in it together while we're in it separately, something like that. I don't see architecture as a different voices option. In other words, Molly Bloom could be Penelope. But Joyce controlled all the voices.

Let's say that it would be possible to talk about the truth, and you could get to the truth in architecture.

The Lindblade project for instance. The Tower uses almost everything, exaggerates, contradicts until it explodes; the court yard using almost nothing, implodes.

Let's call the court the Rothko way and the Tower the Penelope way. Most of the work I've done recently has been the everything way – Penelope. Now it's going toward the almost nothing. Maybe you could get down to a 'through the eye of the needle' architecture. Strip it down. I don't trust Mies to explain this. If I could do that, Rothko, but not the modern cliche. Penelope comes easier.

I had to do a speech in memorium of Craig Ellwood the other day. This is not somebody I knew: he died not too long ago. There was a memorial for him, which ended up being a discussion. It was in his Art's Building in Pasadena. Peter Blake and Ray Kappe spoke, and then they asked me if I would speak for a different generation. This is very hard. I mean the worst thing is to try to talk in a circumstance where somebody died. You don't want to go in and start an argument at a memorial.

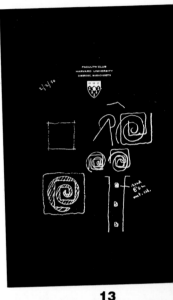

The guy who said it deepest got up and couldn't talk. He was trying to recount his experience with his friend in a way that was not superficial. His instinct was to rip off the surface and get down to the next surface. I was afraid he would rip everything down, have nothing left. Nothing to say. And that's what happened. Everybody was frightened.

Maybe at times there are sensibilities loose in the world. Like one of those flowers you blow on and it goes 'whoosh'. And so it's loose and people are bombarded with the floating petals. I'm not sure who's blowing the flower. Maybe I blow it toward you and you blow it back. Let's say the petals are the Penelope instinct. There are associations developed. Penelope floating everywhere. I think the Rothko instinct should coexist with the Penelope instinct. So Rothko and Penelope could connect, architecture's Yin and Yang. In other words you contain your opposite, but instead of coalescing in a circle . . . the components contest each other. This is what I would like to do, coalescing and attacking. Almost everything and almost nothing. This sounds OK to me, it sounds like something that would always make sense.

I was reading *US News* and *World Report* about physicists looking for the theory of everything. To account for everything. That instinct is always there. The Babylonian map is that and I think we try to do the same, and everybody tries to redraw the map, to account again for what happened and what's happening now and what will happen in the future. Funny thing about maps. If you look at a map of California, it says here's Santa Barbara, here's Fresno, here's Bakersfield. But the map doesn't actually tell you what it's like to be there. So the map is cerebral. But the experiential quality is not there.

Le Corbusier made that two-headed Dionysus-Apollo drawing. Creation as an outpatient search. It shows the man's conservatism, classicism. His balanced aspiration. I turned the drawing sideways, 90 degrees, so Dionysus is on the bottom. Then I xerox-reduced the Apollo image, so Apollo is a tiny piece floating in the huge Dionysian sea. Let's build that.

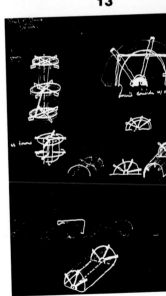

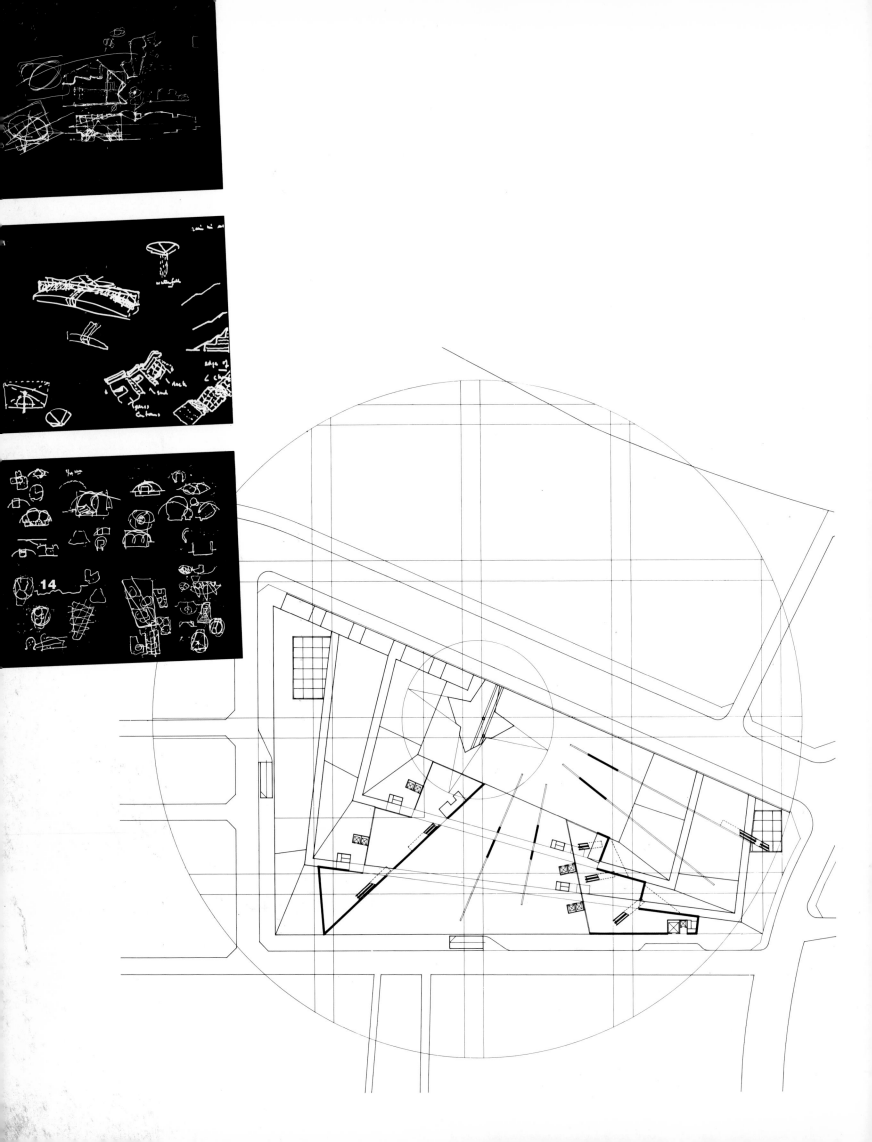

NARA CONVENTION CENTER

'... the great globe itself, Yea all which it
inherit, shall dissolve ...
And like this unsubstantial pageant faded,
Leave not a rack behind.'
The Tempest, Shakespeare

The Nara Convention Center, Japan, has
three components – the Plaza Building
(earth), the Roof Building (sky) and the
Theatre Building (bridge between) – each
of which has both organisational and
philosophical roles in the project concept.

The site, the Plaza Building, is conceived
as an open-air multipurpose plaza and
garden. People may walk singly, or in
groups. Informal and formal talks, open air
assemblies or performances are all accom-
modated and the space facilitates large-
scale exhibits of commercial or industrial
products, paintings or sculpture. The plaza
includes a commemoration of the 1,300
year-old Buddhist origins of Nara.

The plaza is carved into the earth,
offering several levels of walks and gardens, and a variety of spatial experiences.
Major access/egress points occur at the
corners of the site. From the Sanjo-
Honmachi line one enters the plaza directly
at the south end; from the Shibatsuji-
Ohmori line one enters the park directly at
the north-west corner. Vehicles enter from
the west and north. A sub-plaza structure
contains parking, support space for the
theatres and two skylit cafes.

The Roof Building, raised above the
plaza, contains a two-level, four-way
pedestrian street, a theoretical extension of
the city grid. The grid reassociates the
Convention Hall site with the circulation
order of the city. The grid suggests a
reconnected movement system uniting
Convention Hall, the redevelopment site,
and the old city.

In the quadrants, formed by the Roof
Building street-grid, are a restaurant and
bar, galleries and administrative offices.
The theatre structures intervene in the Roof
Building, as they do in the Plaza Building.
From the grid one looks at the garden plaza
below and, on occasion, into the theatres.

The Theatre Buildings form a conceptual
and physical bridge between the Roof and
Plaza Buildings. The theatre structure
originates as a parabolic curve, derived
from viewing angle optimums for seats.
Theatres are raised on legs above the plaza
to approximately street level and are
entered from either of two lobby buildings
providing vertical circulation between plaza
and roof functions.

Lobby buildings are accessed directly
from the street, the plaza, or from the
parking area below. Pedestrians in the
garden/plaza circulate below the theatres
in a landscape that combines greenery,
exhibits, cafes, the stone-paved plaza
punctuated by concrete legs supporting
the theatres and steel columns holing the
Roof Building.

Symbolically, the roof (a portion of a
globe) suggests a primitive, idealised form
of both earth and sky. The building is a
theoretical sphere. But the sphere is
modified to accommodate the specifics of
the city, the programme, and the site. So
the project is simultaneously a theoretical
and a pragmatically amended form.

The top of the globe is the curved roof
form. The apex is cut off above the required
height. The circular plan of the globe
appears literally in the project only where it
crosses the south-east corner of the site.
The theoretical perimeter of the circle (as it
traverses the city beyond the Convention
Center site) defines a limit, a perimeter
for extending the grid in the air, as it
reconnects with the JR Nara Station, the
station plaza and the surrounding
redevelopment area.

The Nara Convention Center's three
pieces – the Roof Building (sky), the Plaza
Building (earth) and the Theatre Building
(bridge) – form and formed by the dissolv-
ing globe, will move Nara through the past
into the future.

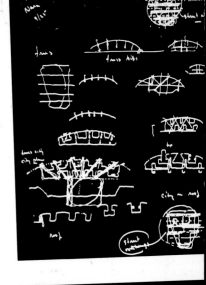

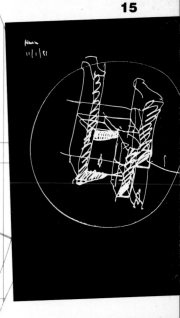

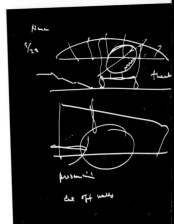

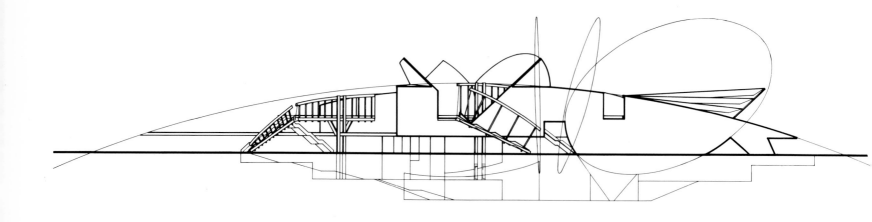

16

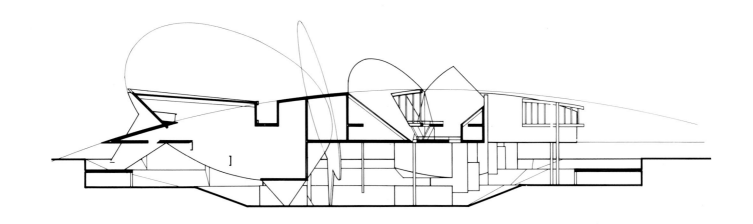

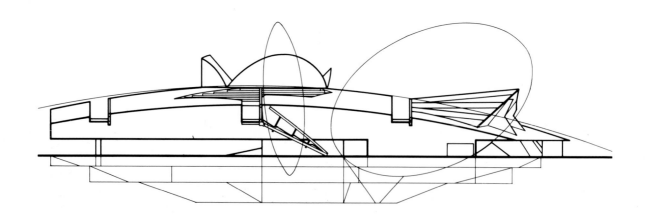

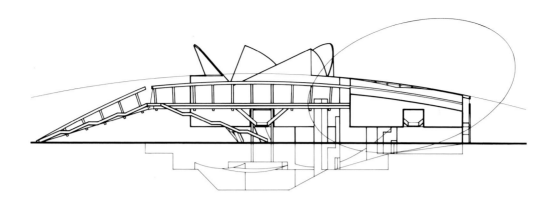

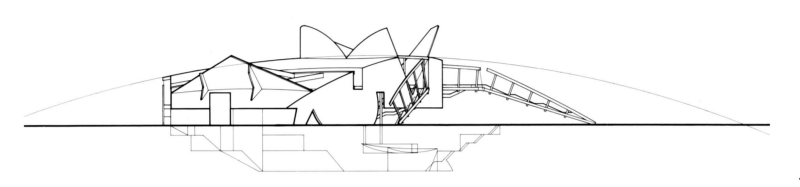

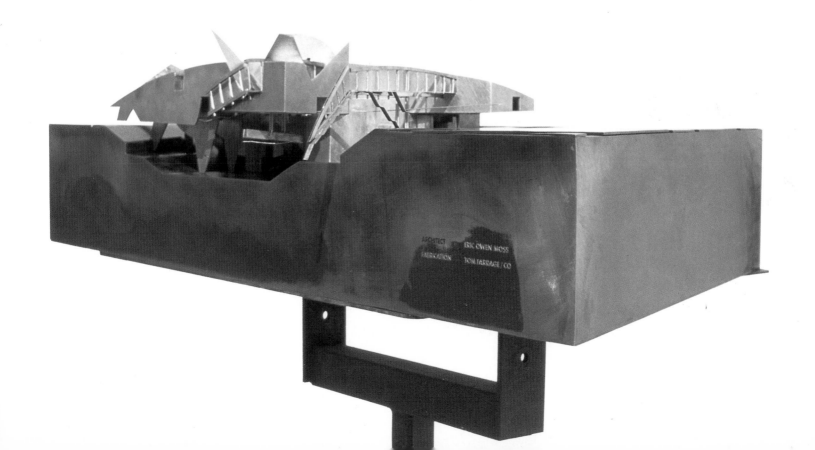

18

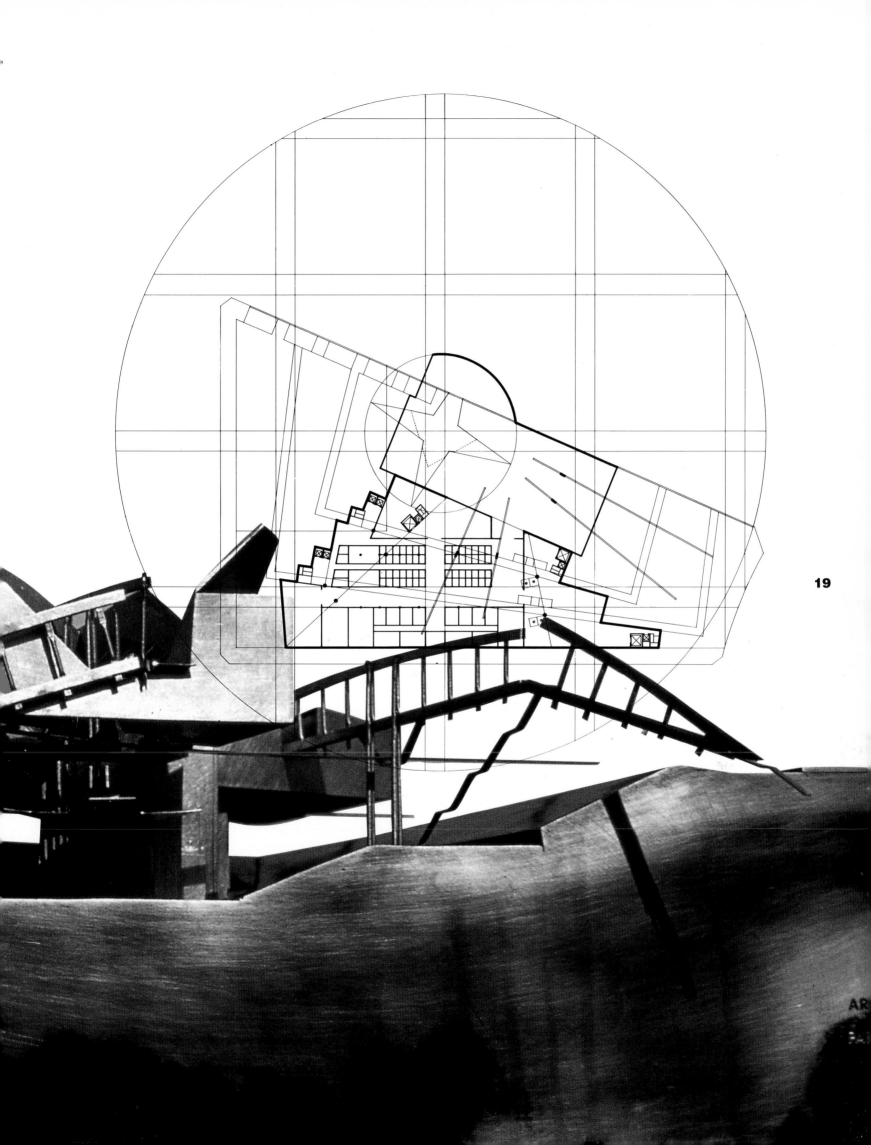

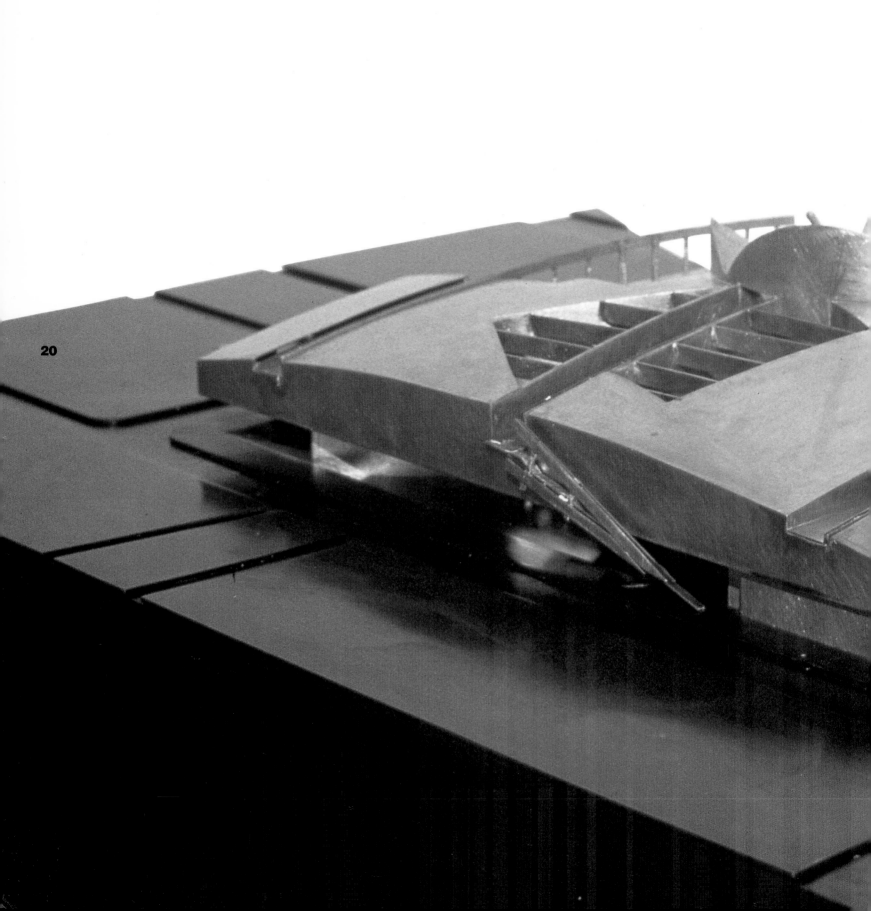

20

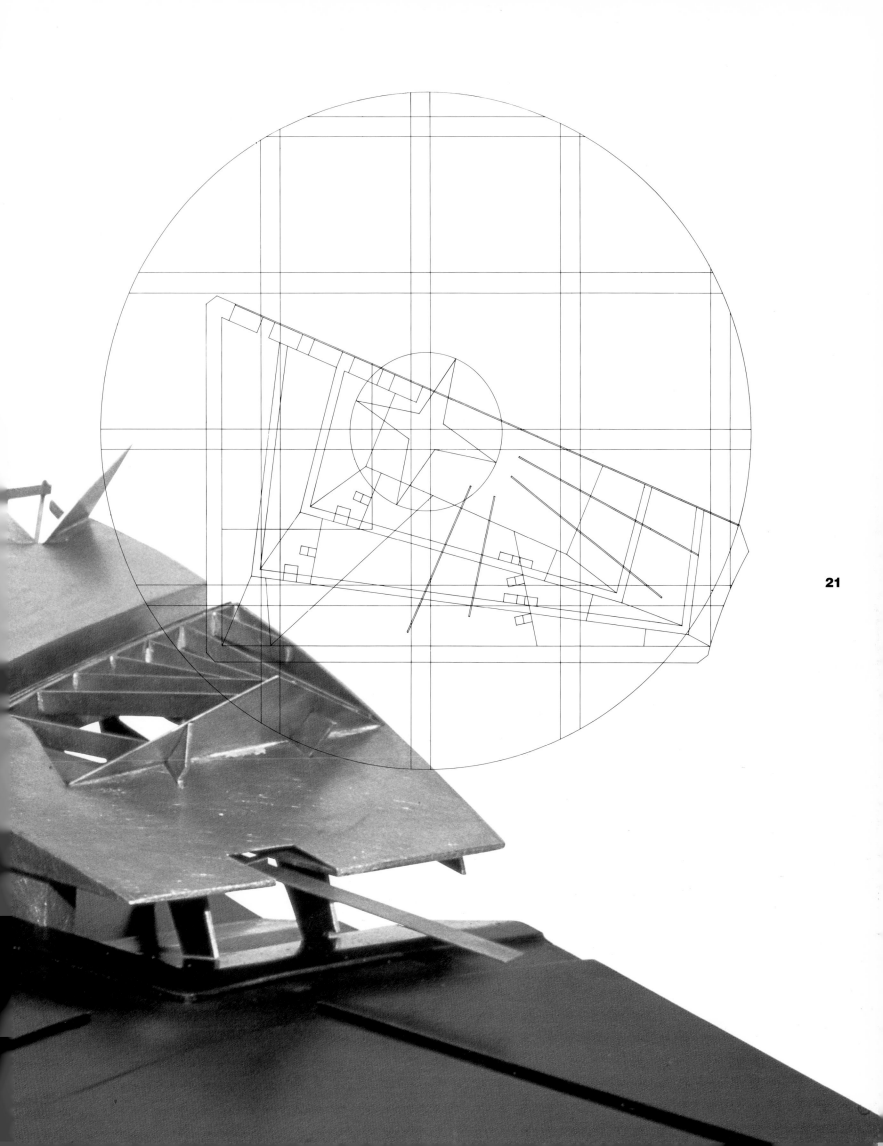

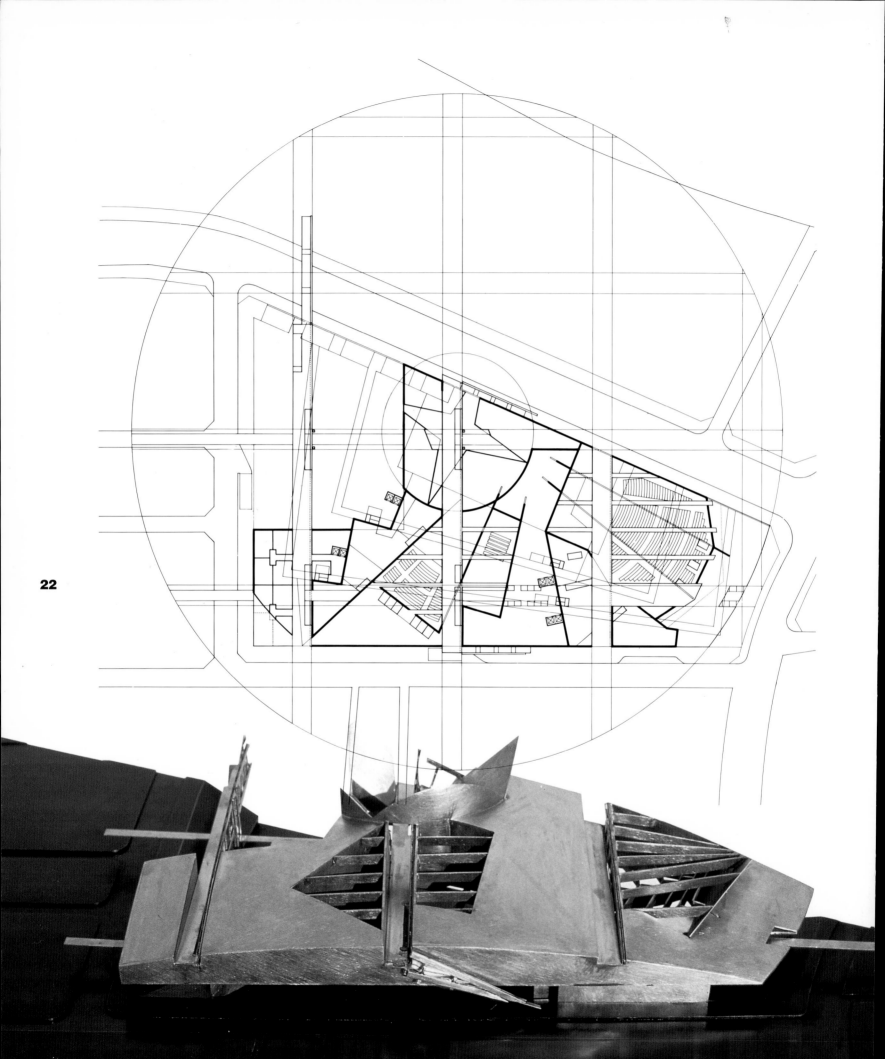

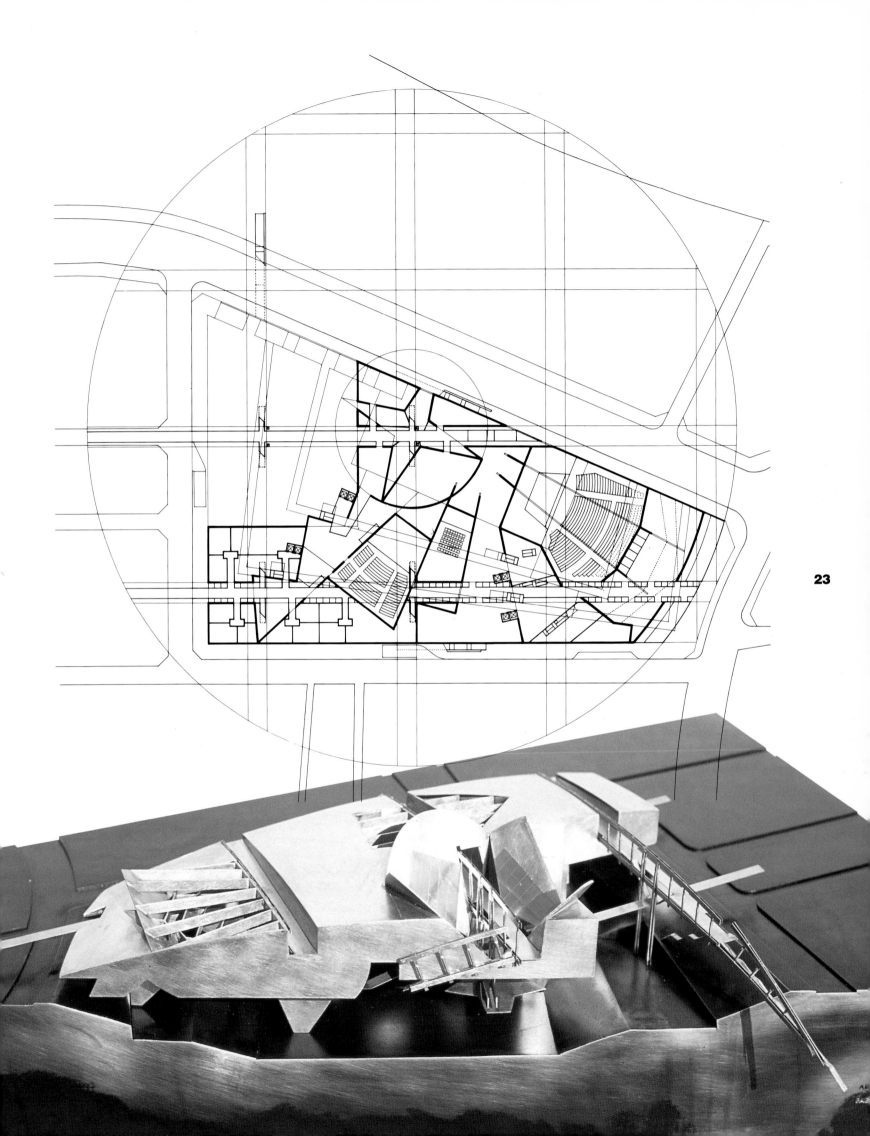

INCE
PARAMOUNT
LAUNDRY BUILDING

A 20,000 square foot warehouse, built in 1940, with poured concrete walls and wood truss supported roof, is located in a Culver City neighbourhood of studio production facilities. This original building had two essential organisational components: firstly, a two-floor perimeter and secondly, an open, double-height volume, centrally positioned in plan with clerestory windows and spanned by wood trusses. Parking requirements permitted a maximum addition of 6,000 square feet to the building. Expansion took place by extending the existing second floor south and by adding a new two-part third floor.

The building is currently occupied by a major Los Angeles graphics design firm, and is approached from the north, via the Santa Monica Freeway from which it can be clearly seen. A new canopy and central lobby are positioned on the street elevation. The lobby is capped with a simple vault, adjusted in plan towards the direction of freeway view and traffic flow. This plan adjustment generates a modified vault in section which is extended above the old roof, identifying the new components of the building below.

This modified roof vault is positioned over the entrance lobby (which contains stairs to the second and third floors), above a bridge and over a new rear exit stair. Where the vault is inserted, the existing roof sheathing is removed and the vault and supporting walls extend vertically above the original roof, visible from the floors below.

The new second floor projects into the central space and is supported by columns which also support the bridge. The new third floor consists of separate areas placed at opposite ends of the central volume. This two-part third floor occurs just below the bottom chord of the existing wood trusses. The two third floors are then linked by a bridge. To allow for vertical clearance in the bridge area, a four-foot portion of the bottom chord of the existing trusses is removed, and restructured with a steel tube below and two new vertical chords.

At the centre of the bridge are two benches, one on each side, which encourage informal meetings or gatherings. The bridge is aligned with the new vaulted roof which allows natural light through new clerestory windows to the bridge from the north.

The building is a combination of wood, steel and reinforced concrete construction. The vault is covered with galvanised sheets

of steel. The new columns supporting the entry canopy and the bridge are vitrified clay pipes filled with reinforced concrete.

Owner: Frederick Norton Smith
Primary Tenant: Sussman/Prejza & Company, Inc
Structural Engineer: Joe Kurily, Kurily Szymanski Tchirkow
Mechanical Engineer: Paul Antieri, I & N Consulting Engineers
Electrical Engineer: Michael Cullen, California Associated Power
General Contractor: Scott Gates Construction Company, Inc
Landscape Architect: Steven Ormenyi, Steven Ormenyi & Associates

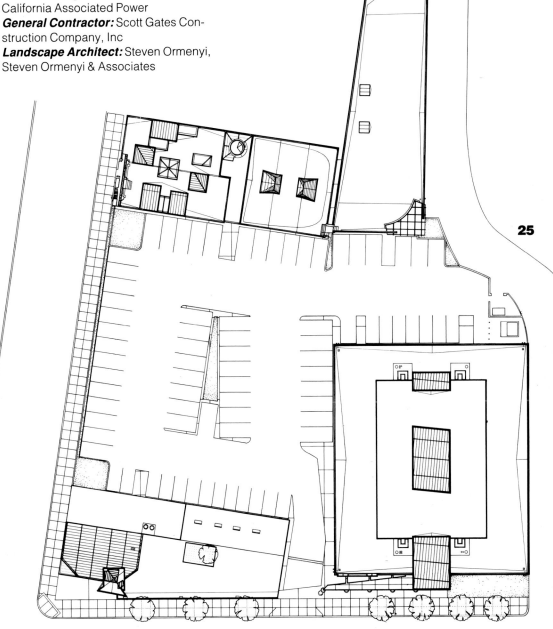

26

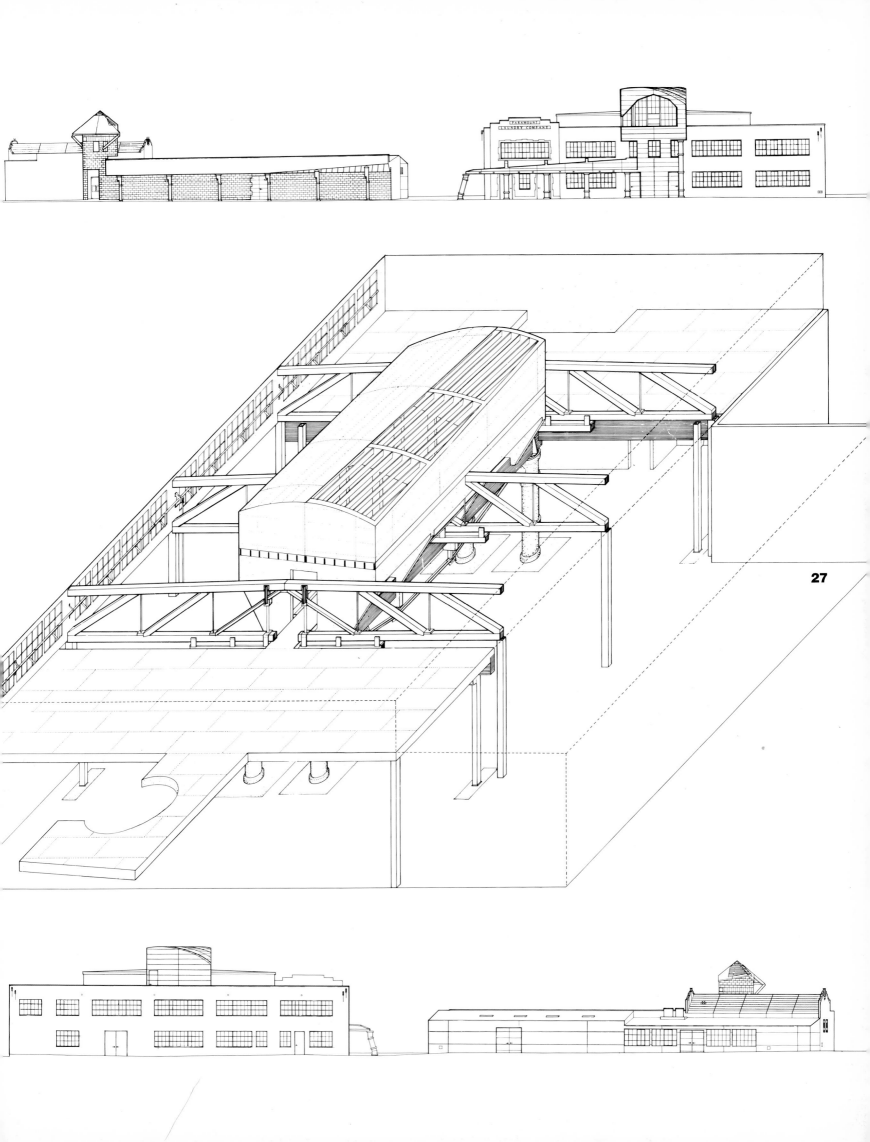

27

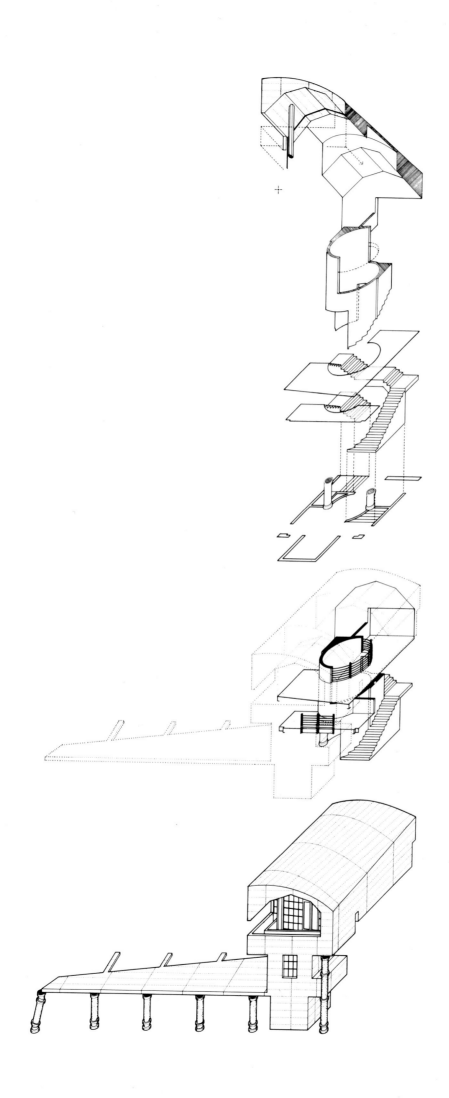

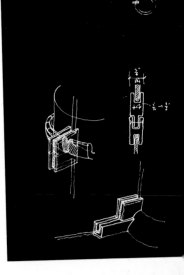

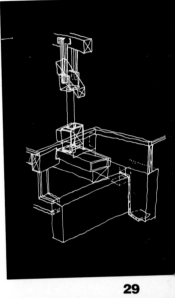

29

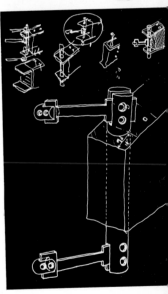

30

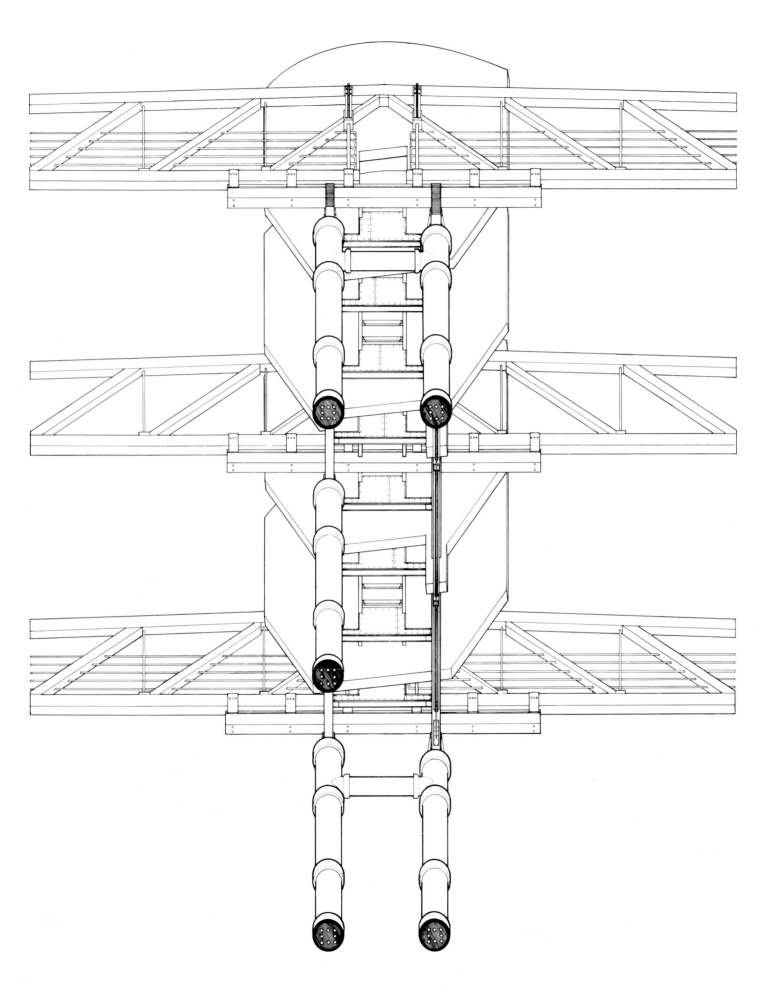

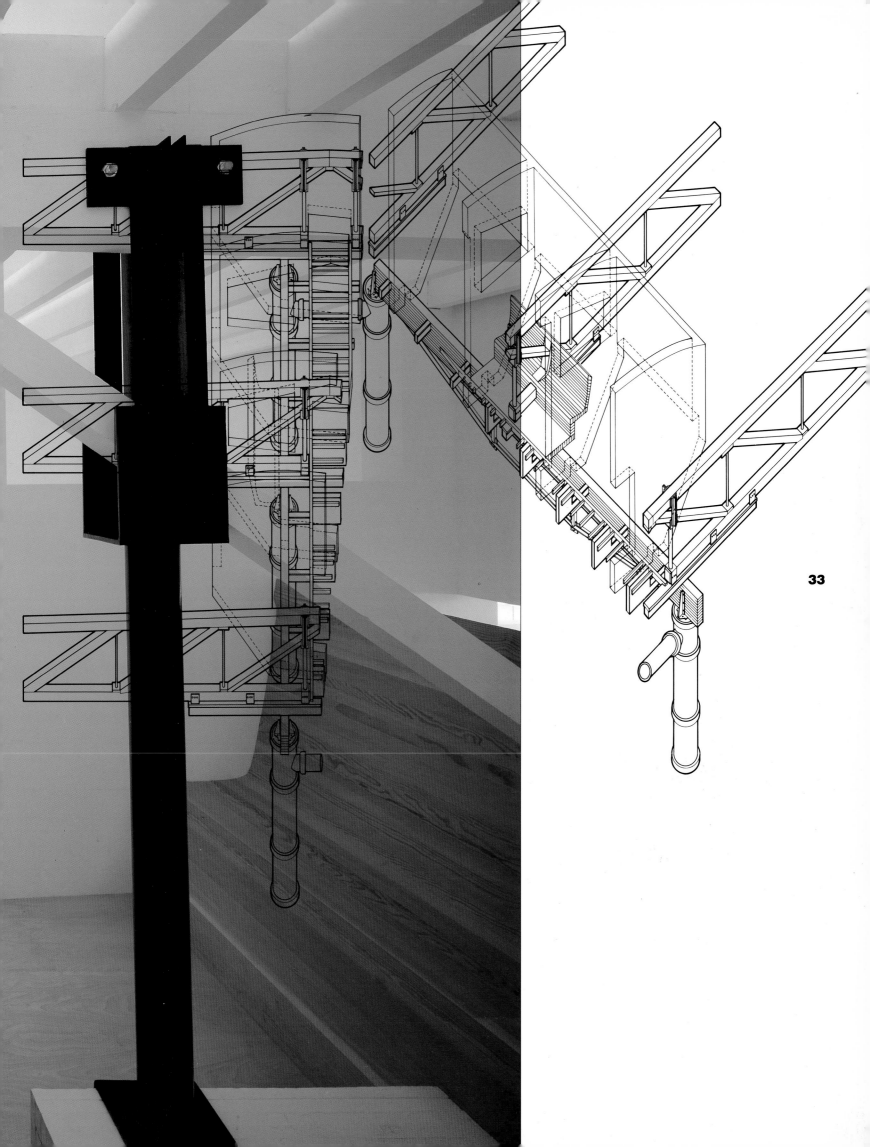

33

INCE
LINDBLADE TOWER

A dilapidated warehouse originally built in the early 1940s in Culver City has been remodelled. The new facility provides a flexible work space for a local graphics company. The exterior wall of an adjoining office has also been remodelled.

Windows are minimised. Two skylights and a courtyard, with a roll-up glass door, provide natural light and air.

The company intends to continuously modify the use of the interior as new projects require. The high, truss supported roof at the north end will contain moveable tables for layouts. Conference tables can also be arranged for open meetings and reviews of work in progress. The remainder of the space will utilise desks, tables, benches and shelves: movable work stations of various kinds. Power, telephone and computer terminals are located at close intervals in walls and floors. Office furnishings can be removed and tables arranged for catered meals. De-mountable partitions could be installed if needed. Two bathrooms are provided. At the south end is a large roll-up door enclosing a storage area the width of the space.

The tower provides a formal entry. A secondary service entrance is provided in the west wall behind the clay colonnade. The tower also signals the buildings' presence to a primary commercial street and Santa Monica Freeway to the north.

A split-one face red concrete block was used to construct the tower and a portion of the street wall. The remaining walls are wood studs covered with a steel trowelled cement plaster finish inside and outside. Original wood trusses supporting the north end roof were repaired and re-used. The roof of this area is a modified 'standing seam', galvanised steel sheet. A portion of the tower roof is open to a glass skylight positioned inside the tower at the section line of the steel panelled roof. Where the tower roof opens to the skylight below, wood roof beams are covered with galvanised steel. Where the tower roof is closed,

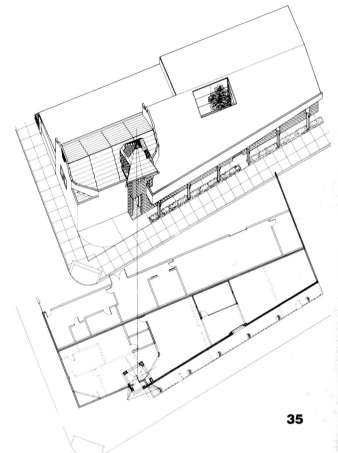

the roof is a factory painted white steel. A line of vitrified clay covered reinforced concrete columns fronts the main street. The exterior wall of the adjacent office space is 24 x 4 foot sheets of bonded epoxy and wood particles (strand board), covered with a clear grey sealer. The two spaces share a common interior wall, also of strand board. The new bathroom space, with HVAC units above, is galvanised steel sheets over wood studs.

The HVAC system is composed of two gas fired high efficiency furnaces, two high efficiency condensers and two electronically programmable thermostats with remote sensors for energy conservation.

This building provides conservation of existing building scale and type, modified for both a new external identity and a flexible interior for a new user.

Owner: Frederick Norton Smith
Structural Engineer: Gordon Polon, The Office of Gordon Polon
Mechanical Engineer: Greg Tchamitchian, AEC Systems
Electrical Engineer: Michael Cullen, California Associated Power
General Contractor: Scott Gates, Construction Company, Inc
Landscape Architect: Steven Ormenyi, Steven Ormenyi & Associates

35

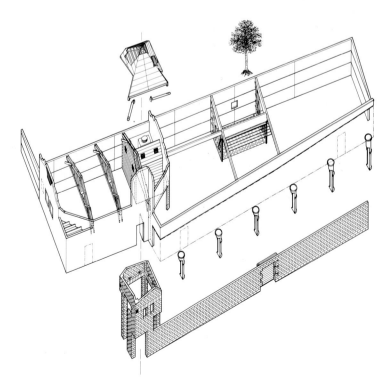

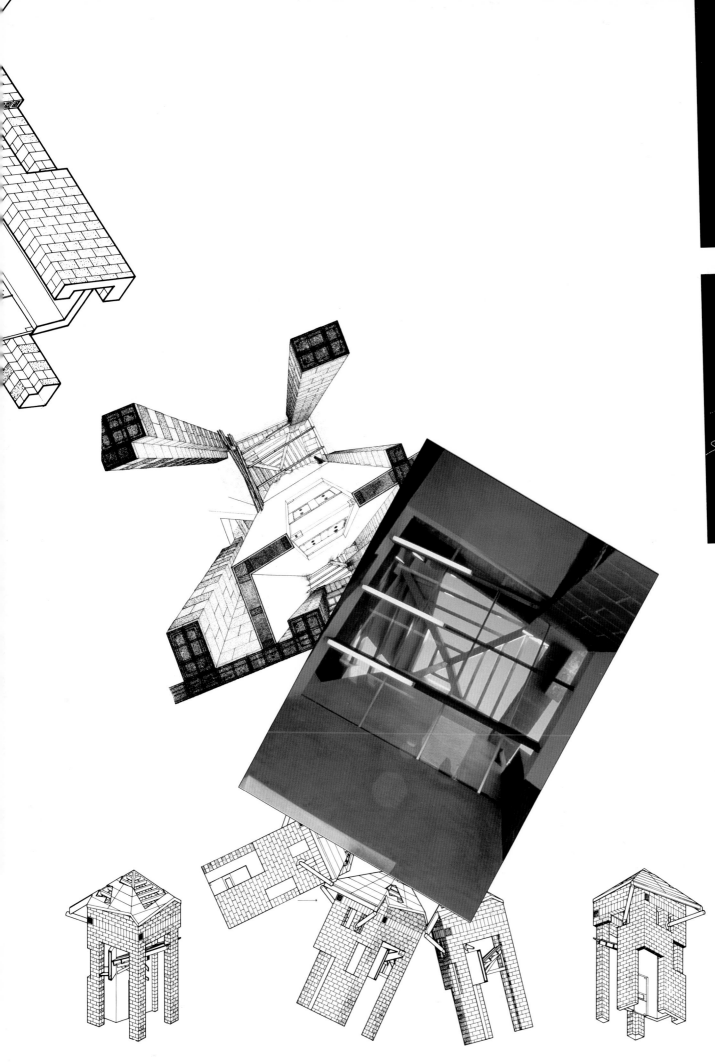

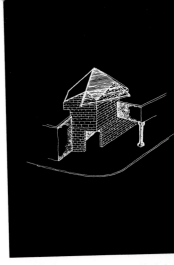

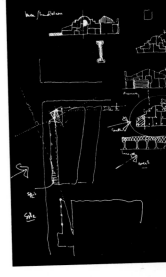

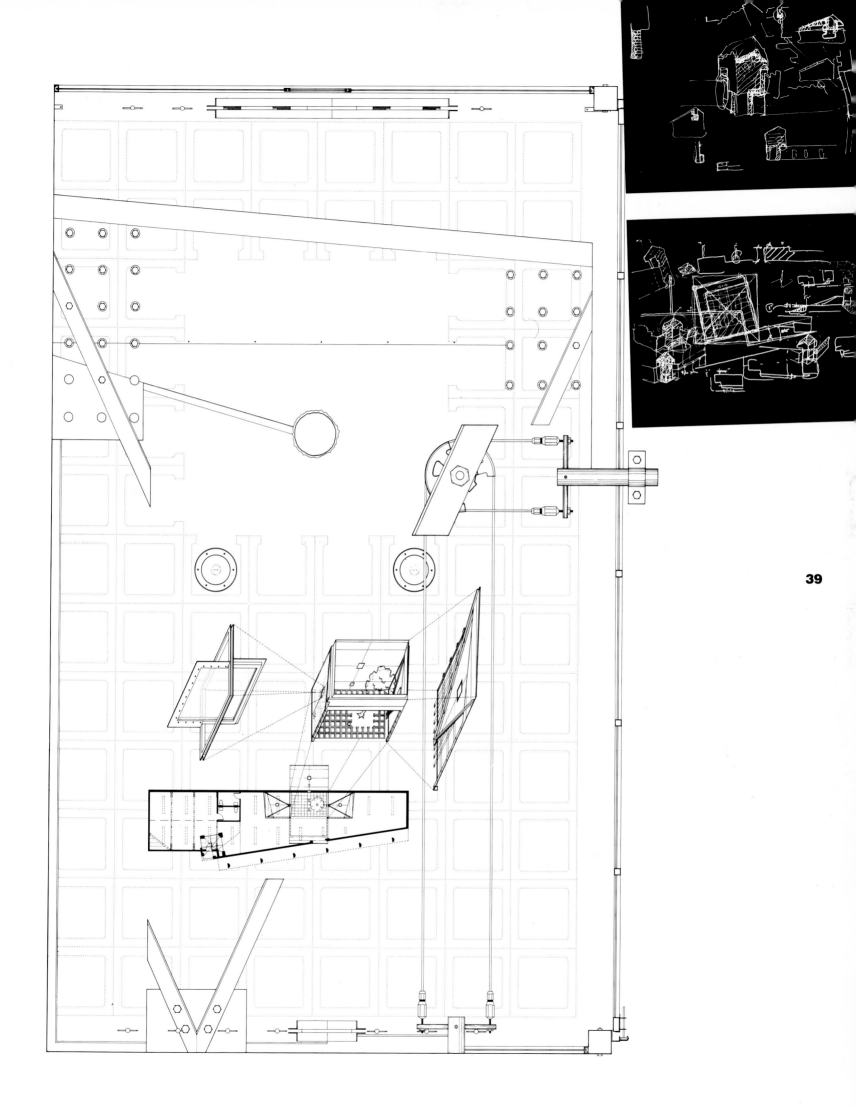

GARY GROUP OFFICE BUILDING

The Gary Group Office Building is the third portion of a four building office complex in Culver City, California, involving both new construction and remodelling. The first two buildings: Paramount Laundry and Lindblade Tower, totalling 40,000 square feet, are completed and occupied. The result has been a significant revitalisation of a deteriorating area.

The Gary Group is an advertising and promotion agency specialising in the fields of entertainment and leisure. Its building is conceived as a picaresque novel with a series of discontinuous adventures involving the same participants. The novel can be opened at any point and read either forwards or backwards.

The building has two entrances. One, facing the one-way street just north of the project, is cut from an almost free-standing concrete block wall inclined to the leeward, resting on 'C' shaped steel ribs implanted in an adjoining wall. A clock, perhaps legible, is attached to the west end of the inclined wall, facing the car park. The second entrance, cut in a wall embellished with chains, wires, pipes, re-bar, block planters and flowers, confronts the car park.

Inside, immediately south of the inclined wall, is a group of work stations arranged within a sometime cruciform plan/gable section. Work stations mix with four tiny landscaped courtyards. At the centre is a pool, open to the sky. Adjoining this area is a hall terminated by a private meditation room. A conical steel cap, supported on legs of wood and steel, punctures a half-pyramid skylight that roofs the room. South of the hall is a two-storey area that includes both private offices and open counters for graphic artists. The vaulted roof, supported by two bowstring trusses, is carefully interrupted by two enormous aluminium, glass and sheet metal funnels that deposit natural light inside.

41

Owner: Frederick Norton Smith
Tenant: The Gary Group
Steel Furniture Fabricator: Tom Farrage, Farrage & Co
Structural Engineer: Gary Davis, Davis Design Group
Mechanical Engineer: Greg Tchamitchian, AEC Systems
Electrical Engineer: Michael Cullen, California Associated Power
General Contractor: Jamik, Inc
Construction Manager: Leonard Bass, AJ Contracting of California, Inc
Lighting Designer: Saul Goldin, Saul Goldin and Associates

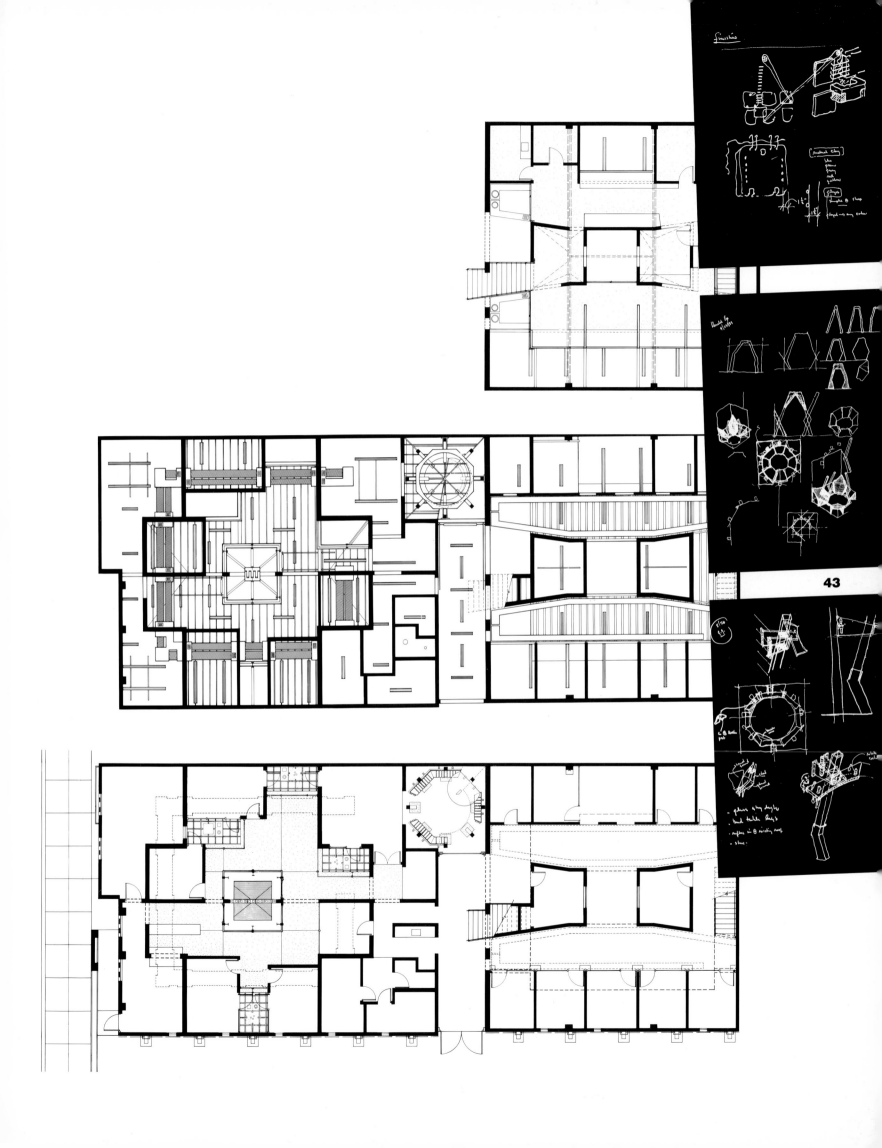

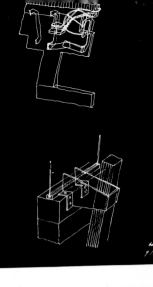

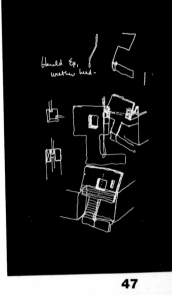

47

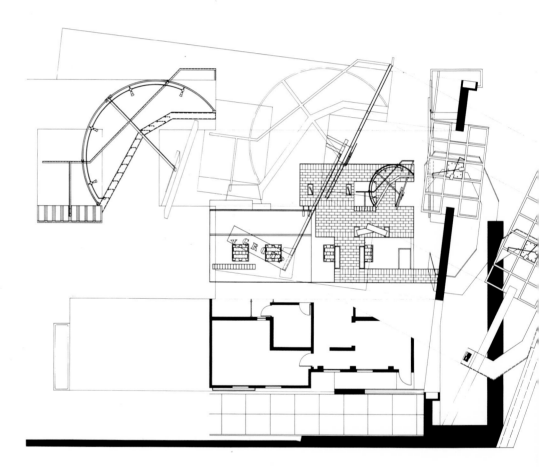

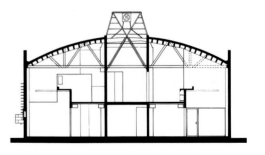

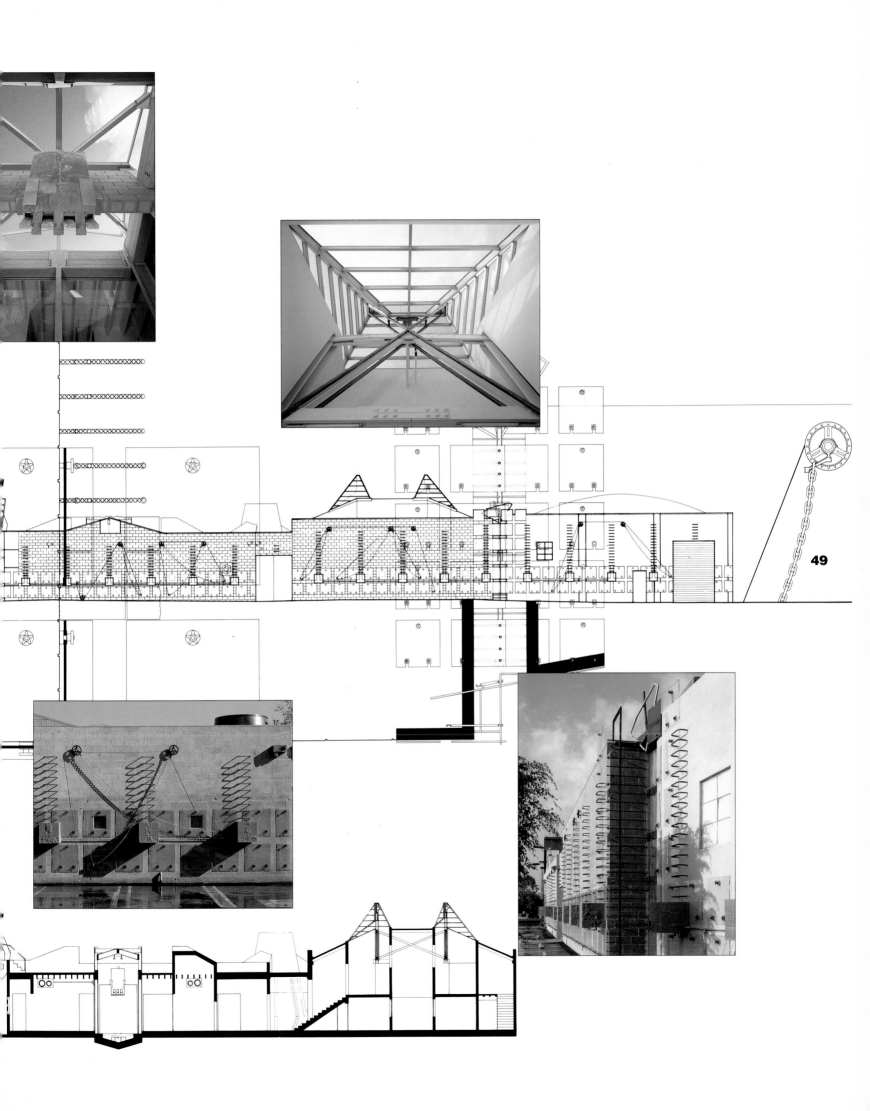

INCE
GEM

GEM is the fourth piece of the Ince Complex. The building contains the offices of the entertainment media company of GEM/ Fattal & Collins.

The existing shell is a 9,000 square feet tilt-up concrete warehouse, trapezoidal in plan, framed with bowstring trusses.

The essential architectural event occurs at the south-west corner, a hybrid conjunction of a 12-sided figure, the trapezoidal plan, the bowstring roof and a theoretical sphere. Operationally, the space contains a stairway that connects the lobby with the second-floor bridge. The balance of the building contains two floors of private and semi-private offices and support space.

To the north, paraphernalia on the west face of the Gary Group building extends along the front facade of GEM, an almost continuous elevation bracketed by the GEM corner and the Gary Group clock.

50

51

52

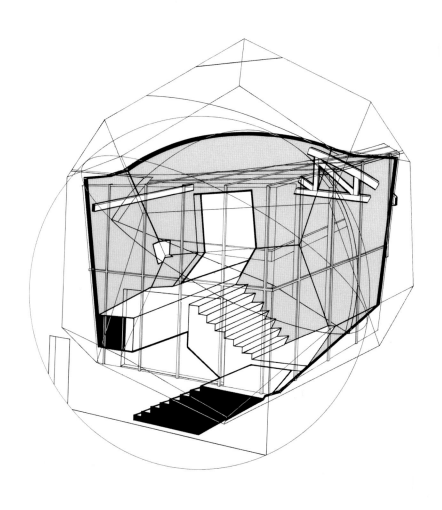

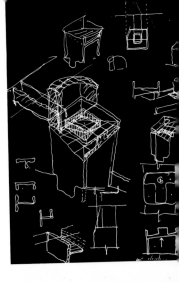

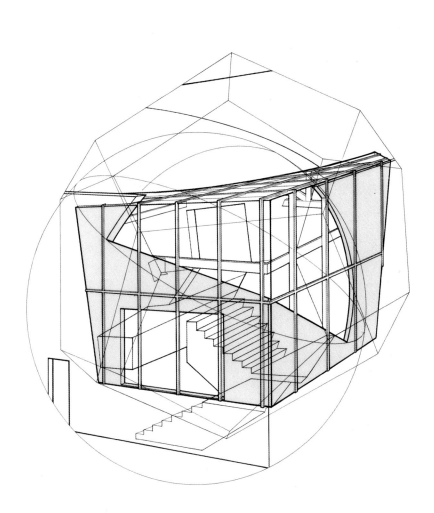

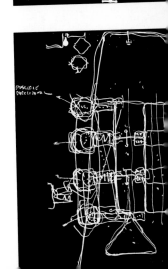

56

MAK TERRACE
PLATEAU

The Austrian Museum for Applied Arts
(Osterreichisches Museum für Angewandte
Kunst) constructed a concrete platform
cantilevered over a pedestrian walkway
and canal in the First District.

   The strategy is to build a theatre, open to
the city and sky. A cylindrical stair,
punched through a circular cut in the deck,
connects the terrace with the canal walkway below.

   Above the circular hole, two intersecting
steel ribs, conceptually identical, wrap the
space without enclosing it. The rib eleva-
tions are bridge analogues, structure
climbing over itself, bridges from nowhere
to nowhere.

   Each of the ribs is curtailed, amended by
existing constraints. Bleachers are hung
from the ribs.

   In the end there are only pieces, pieces
of round. There is no effort to suggest a
unity, chronology, or sequence.

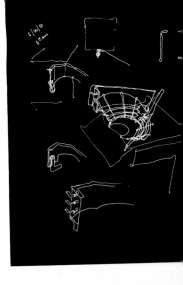

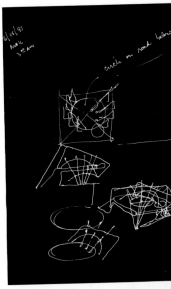

57

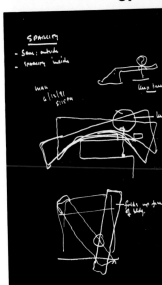

58

60

8522 NATIONAL BOULEVARD COMPLEX
OFFICE BUILDING

On National Boulevard, a main thorough-fare in Culver City, California, five ware-houses adjoin one another, to form a single building. The first building was constructed in the 1920s and the others followed during the 30s and 40s. All were long span spaces with clerestory windows facing either east or north. There was never any attempt to co-ordinate the design of the earlier building with the later ones. Buildings were simply added as additional square footage was required. By 1986, the building – used as a plastics factory – was filled with partitions, hung ceilings, ducts, sprinkler lines and rooms of every size. The exterior was dilapidated.

The owner decided to have the building re-constituted and make it available for commercial use. A steel canopy was stretched across the street elevation, propped on struts extended from the existing wall. An elliptical entry court was cut into the original building, exposing a piece of truss structure to the street. The wall of the ellipse is constructed of concrete block, and both truss and ellipse are partially covered with steel.

A pedestrian entry ramp from the street leads into the court, then through the entry door to a causeway organised around an existing column system. The hallway wall consists of three pieces: a frame wall of painted dry-wall, an arch wall of speckled blue plaster and a glass wall, which occurs occasionally.

The causeway leads to a middle lobby, newly skylit, with a perimeter wall of block and plaster. This lobby is related in plan form to the entry ellipse.

Turning south, there is a second cause-way which leads to a large meeting room. A third ellipse (inclined in section) has been built into an existing room with walls of concrete block. The original block is some-times painted, sometimes sandblasted.

The new meeting room walls are birch plywood, attached to the studs with brass screws. These studs are partially exposed to reveal the mechanism by which the room was constructed. The ceiling is plastered, while the floor is the original concrete.

The causeway and lobby organisation allows the owner to sub-divide and lease to a number of tenants in a variety of ways or to simply lease to a single tenant.

Owner: Frederick Norton Smith
Structural Engineer: Gordon Polon, The Office of Gordon Polon
Mechanical Engineer: Paul Antieri, I & N Consulting Engineers
Electrical Engineer: Paul Immerman, I & N Consulting Engineers
Lighting Consultant: Saul Goldin, Saul Goldin and Associates
General Contractor: Kevin Kelly

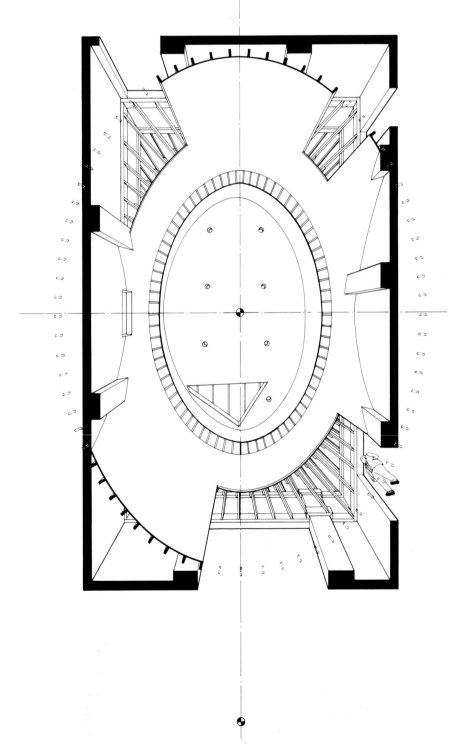

61

62

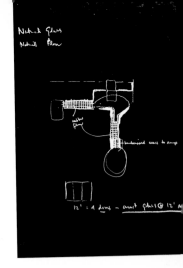

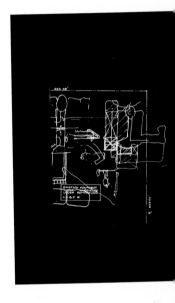

63

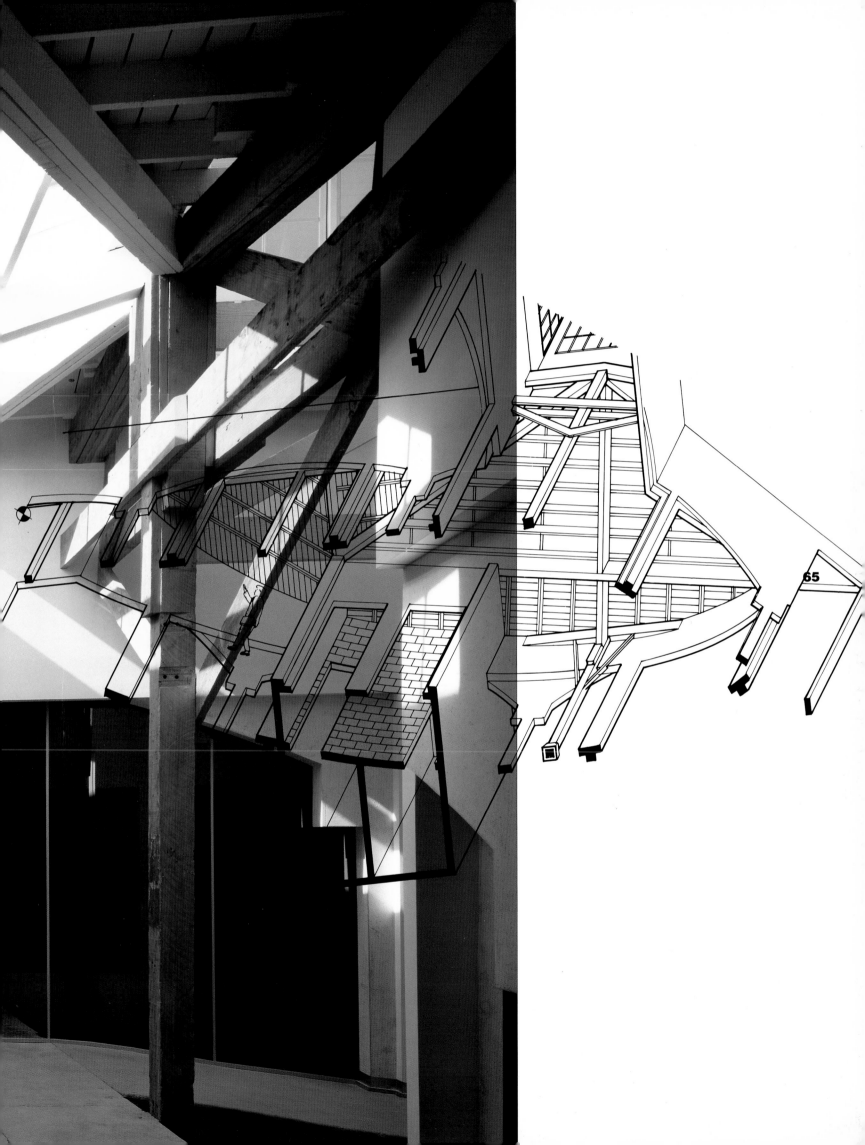

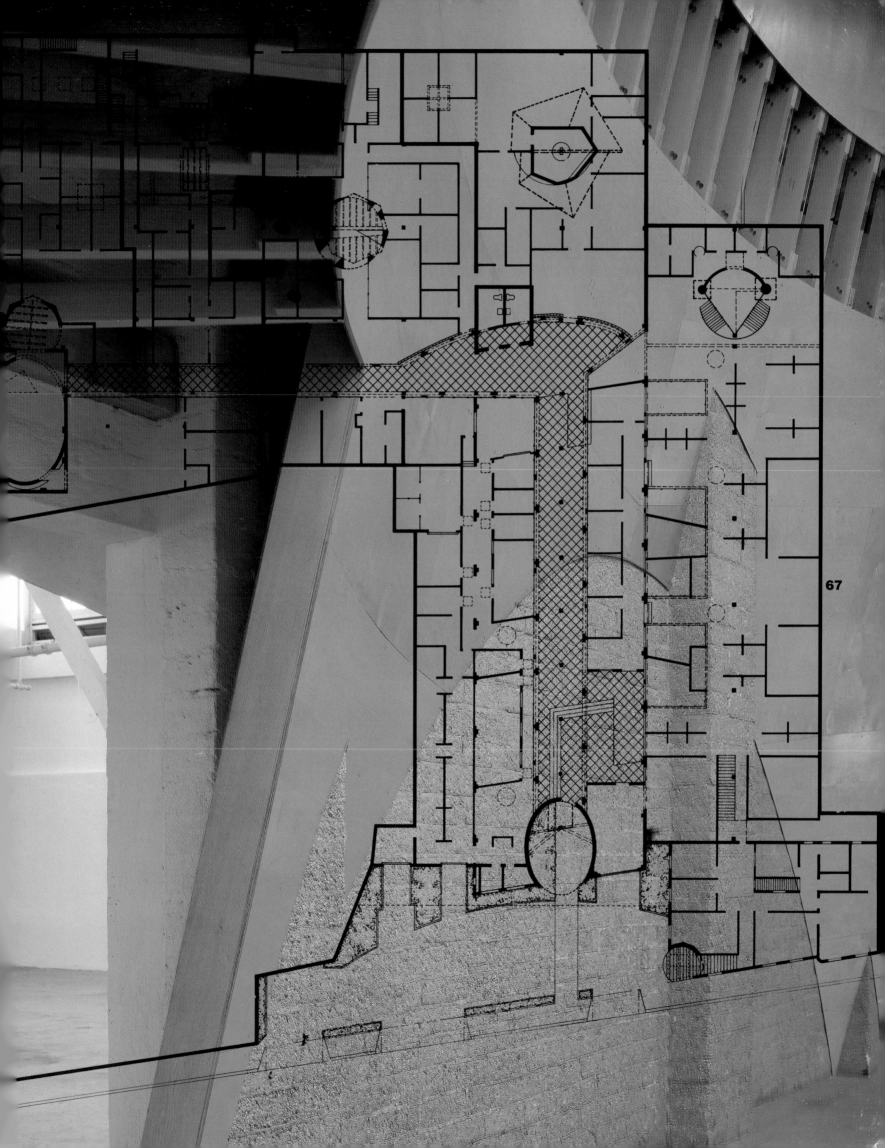

67

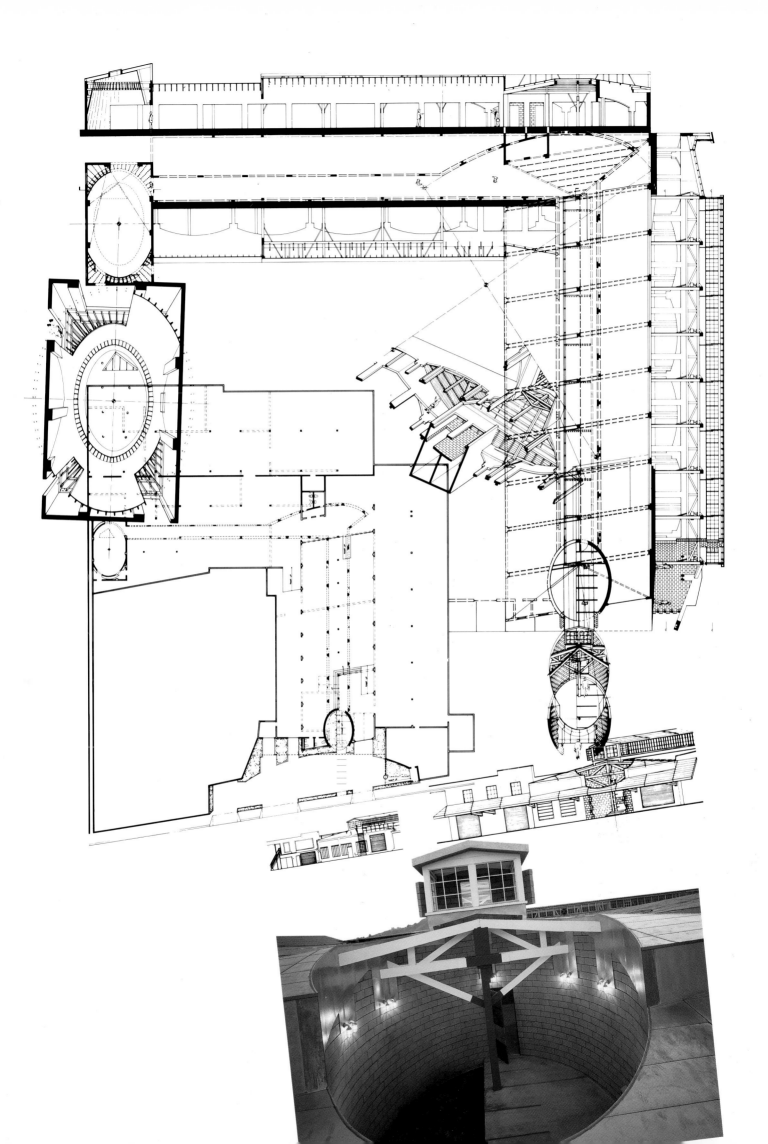

8522 NATIONAL BOULEVARD COMPLEX
SMA OFFICES

SMA, a design firm specialising in video graphics, occupies 16,000 square feet of the 8522 National Boulevard Office Building shell. The conceptual framework of this project is a central causeway, 175 feet long, anchored at the west end by an exercise room and on the east end by a stairwell. At the opposite end, the central walk connects with two floors of executive offices and conference space.

The causeway perimeter is defined by fully enclosed offices on the south and partially enclosed work areas to the north. South offices are glazed to seven feet, and then dry-wall to the ceiling above. Work areas are dry-wall to seven feet, then hyperbolic wood frame lids open to a clerestory window on the north wall. The hyperbolic lid is generated by a horizontal line parallel to the top of the dry-wall at one edge and the sloping sill of the clerestory glass at the other.

The causeway itself follows an original line of wood post supports and connecting beams running the length of the space. Steel angles are bolted to both sides of the wood beams, aligned with lasers, and shimmed to form a precise organisational reference line to which all additional components conform. To this central beam tapered steel ribs, 'T' shaped in cross section, are attached. Two types of hangers are also connected to the reference beam, one which supports the HVAC ducts, another which supports steel boxes containing power, computer and communication lines. Air, heat, light, power and communications are supplied to office and work areas with ducts and conduit branches perpendicular to the central frame.

A second line of private offices runs parallel to the causeway with three circulation links to the main walk. These three circulation intersections are defined by stiffening pairs of steel ribs with tubular struts and fastening ribbed acrylic sheets over the ribs. Above the acrylic sheets round domed skylights are positioned.

The interior roof of the exercise room at the west end of the walk is a wood deck from which HVAC units, sitting on adjoining steel columns, are serviced. This deck is accessed by stairs on either side of the exercise room. From the platform a stair provides service access to the roof.

Owner: Frederick Norton Smith
Tenant: SMA
Structural Engineer: Joe Kurily, Kurily Szymanski Tchirkow
Mechanical Engineer: Greg Tchamitchian, AEC Systems
Electrical Engineer: John Silver, Silver, Roth & Associates, Inc
General Contractor: Leonard Bass, A J Contracting of California, Inc
Lighting Designer: Saul Goldin, Saul Goldin and Associates

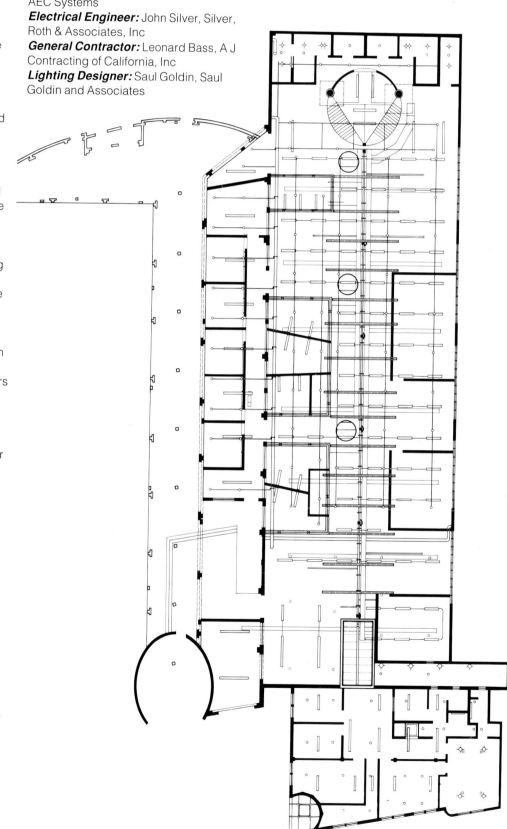

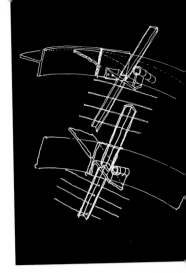
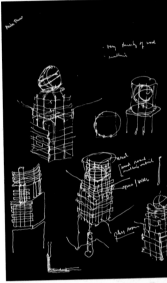

75

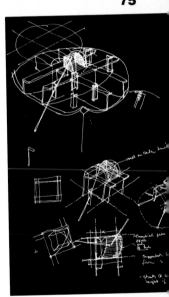

8522 NATIONAL BOULEVARD COMPLEX
QUALITATIVE RESEARCH CENTRE

Qualitative Research Corporation is a consumer affairs research group, whose 4,000 square foot space is entered from a skylit lobby at the junction of two interior pedestrian walks.

The building shell is an old warehouse, remodelled in 1988, with north-easterly oriented saw-tooth skylights and a roof supported by wood trusses. There are no perimeter windows. The programme combines open and closed office space for business activity, graphic design areas, two conference rooms and a library.

The library is the conceptual centre of the project. It is pentagonal in plan, with each external side facing a particular programme use. The pentagon is modified both in plan and section to accommodate programme requirements and the existing construction. At a height of about seven feet the walls splay outward, gathering a maximum of natural light as they intersect the existing saw-tooth roof. A steel table cantilevers from an existing post in the room, and steel shelves hang from two walls. The remaining spaces are arranged orthogonally around the library form.

Two conference rooms adjoin the library on its north side. The first room is used for group interviews by the staff. The second is occupied by clients who overhear and oversee (by means of a one-way mirror) the discussions taking place in room one.

All the finishes are painted dry-wall except the library which is made of cedar particle board panels, both inside and out. The original structure is painted green, and the original ceiling is white.

The furniture is designed specifically for the space. Built-in counters are made of lacquered strand board. One desk for the QRC lobby is cold-rolled steel and glass, the other is of vertical grain fir and cold-rolled steel. The library table is also made of cold-rolled steel.

79

Owner: Federick Norton Smith
Tenant: Qualitative Research Centre, Inc
Structural Engineer: Joe Kurily, Kurily Szymanski Tchirkow
Mechanical Engineer: Greg Tchamitchian, AEC Systems
Electrical Engineer: Mike Cullen, California Associated Power
Lighting Designer: Saul Goldin, Saul Goldin and Associates
General Contractor: Scott Gates, Construction Company, Inc
Furniture Designer: Eric Owen Moss
Furniture Fabricator: Tom Farrage, Farrage & Co

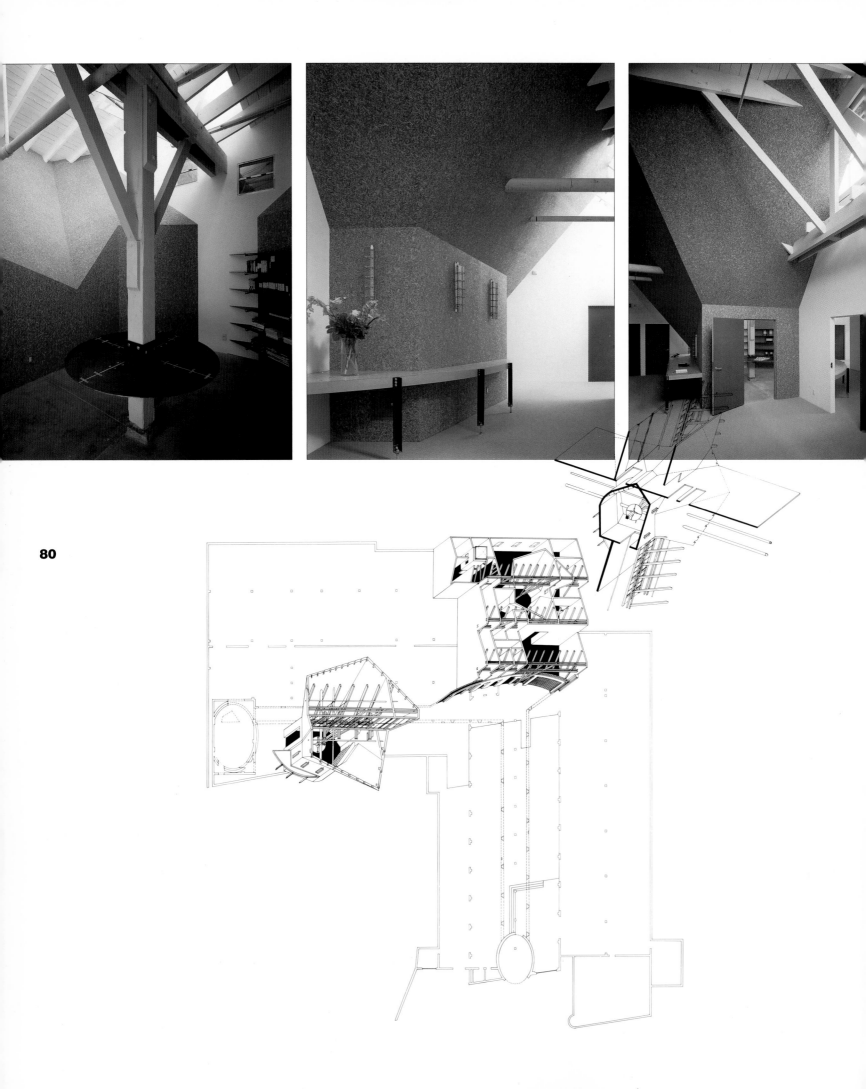

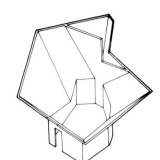

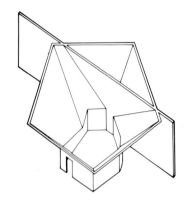

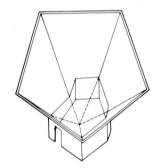

81

8522 NATIONAL BOULEVARD COMPLEX
GOALEN GROUP

The Goalen Group is a film design and production company that occupies 4,500 square feet in the renovated 8522 National Boulevard Office Building.

The original building shell is a wood frame construction with north-east oriented saw-tooth skylights and a wood truss supported roof. There is no perimeter glass. The programme combines open and closed offices, design and film editing space, a conference room, a projection area, a screening room and a kitchen.

The conceptual centre of the project is an exhibition and circulation space, which is steel framed and structurally independent, with three projections through the existing roof. Sign lights mounted on these projections, above the roof, illuminate the area below. The roof of the exhibition space is glazed and the glass conforms to the original saw-tooth profile. A series of steel platforms and shelves are provided for exhibits.

The projection and screening rooms are located at the back of the space beyond the circulation path, which runs from the lobby through the exhibition centre. The screening room seats about 35; seven slide projectors can operate simultaneously. Because of height and projection requirements, the existing shell was demolished to accommodate a new construction for these two rooms. The remainder of the space is an amalgamation of old and new.

Open offices are arranged on the south edge of the central space. On the opposite side, floor to ceiling glass partitions enclose conference and design/editing areas. A second circulation path, at right angles to the first, runs through the central exhibit space, linking the owner's office with the conference room.

All finishes are painted dry-wall except the central space, which is a two colour cement plaster. The original structure is painted green.

Owner: Frederick Norton Smith
Tenant: The Goalen Group
Structural Engineer: Joe Kurily, Kurily Szymanski Tchirkow
Mechanical Engineer: Greg Tchamitchian, AEC Systems
Electrical Engineer: John Silver, Silver, Roth & Associates, Inc
General Contractor: Turner Smith Company
Lighting Designer: Saul Goldin, Saul Goldin and Associates

83

84

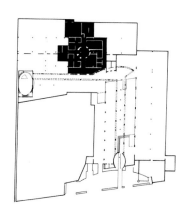

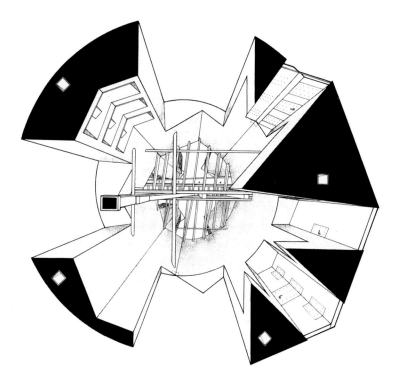

86

Hybrid Arts is involved in the computer digitising of music and the application of computerised sound systems to the audio portion of films.

The company occupies 5,000 square feet in the 8522 National Boulevard Office Building project. Interior spaces are planned to be of two kinds: private office and technical/laboratory space.

The key to the proposed project organisation is a circulation hall which connects the entry lobby with rear offices, labs and conference rooms. Offices are given the greatest visibility, with a glazed perimeter wall separating offices from the major public walk adjacent to the Hybrid Arts space.

Technical/laboratory spaces, located internally on the closed side of the tenant's hallway, have no public visibility.

In order to achieve privacy, the partition separating circulation from office or lab areas is typically cut at eight feet above the floor and enclosed with a wire-glass lid. Utilities run between the glass ceiling and the building roof, extending into work spaces as required.

Office partitions are covered with fibre-glass reinforced concrete board, a construction system conventionally used as a backing for finished panels.

Owner: Frederick Norton Smith
Tenant: Hybrid Arts
Structural Engineer: Joe Kurily, Kurily Szymanski Tchirkow
Mechanical Engineer: Greg Tchamitchian, AEC Systems
Electrical Engineer: Mike Cullen, California Associated Power
Lighting Designer: Saul Goldin, Saul Goldin and Associates
General Contractor: Scott Gates Construction Company, Inc
Furniture Fabricator: Tom Farrage, Farrage & Co

90

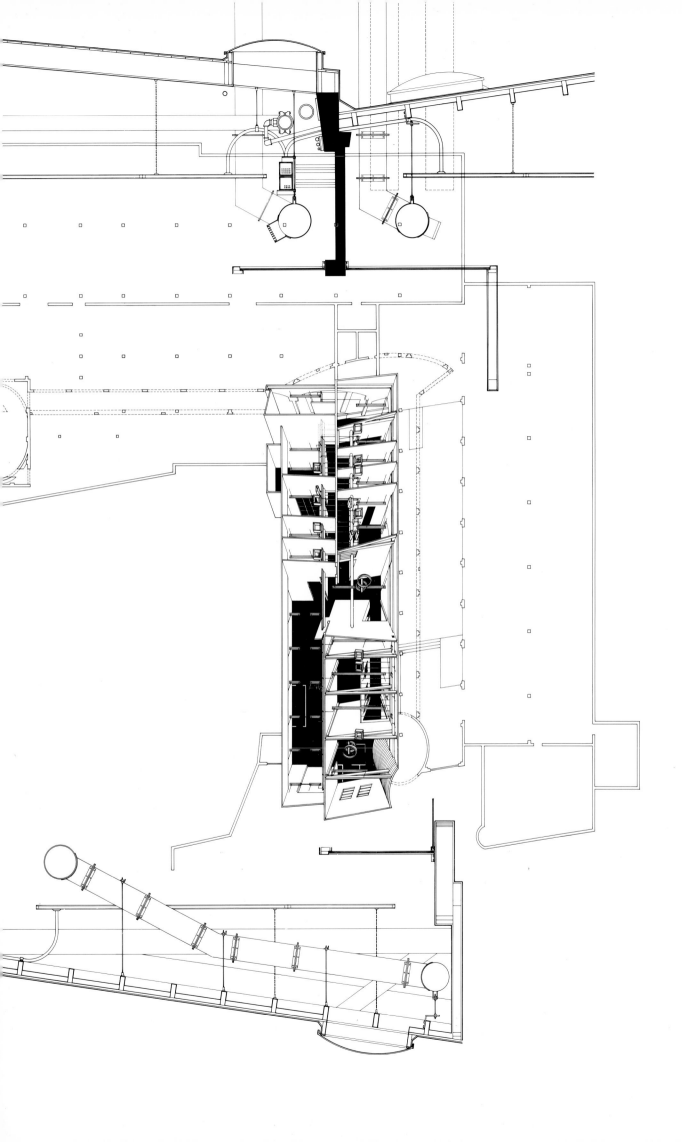

THE BOX

An existing industrial warehouse space, adjacent to 8522 National, will contain a new restaurant, bakery, cafe/coffee bar, corporate offices and a private dining room – the Box. A covered, gazed court is envisaged as the entrance to the restaurant.

Inside the restaurant a system of steel ribs supports a series of wooden screens that separate private dining areas from the public dining space.

The erstwhile orthogonal Box will project from the roof of the existing warehouse. The box is to be supported on steel legs formed around an imaginary globe. The residue of the globe is manifest in the arched beam profiles and two curved steel channels which tie the beams together.

Below the Box is an open deck, defined by the edges of two existing trusses. Below that, within the existing shed, are the bar, cafe and bakery.

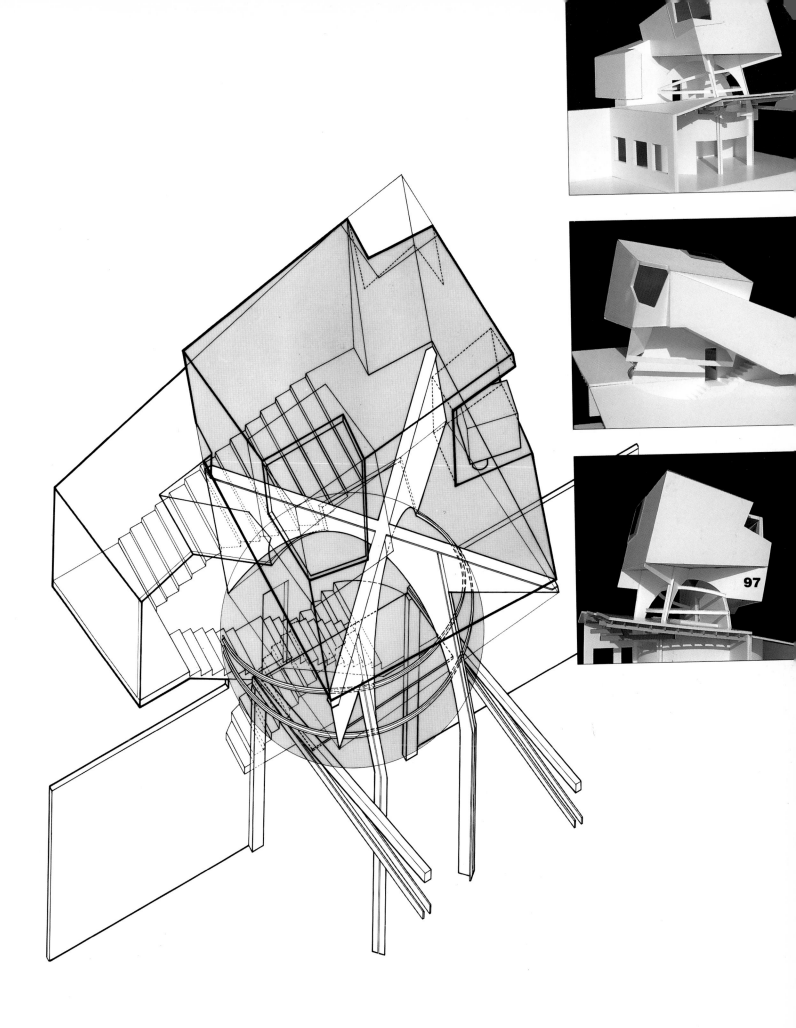

97

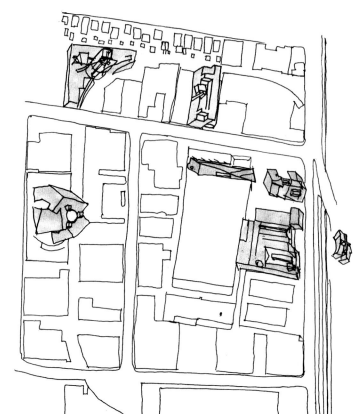

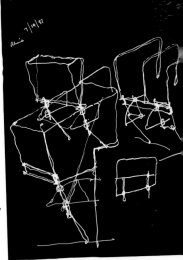

HAYDEN TRACT

The ownership of this portion of Culver City is shared by private developers and public agencies. The general strategy is to identify it as an 'Architectural-free zone'.

The planning and design effort will entirely re-define and re-constitute a dying industrial area. The architect, developer and the city administration are collaborating to invent new urban criteria, free of the conventional antiquated constraints.

It's on the way . . .

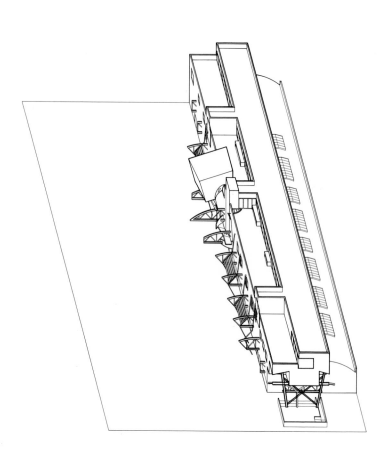

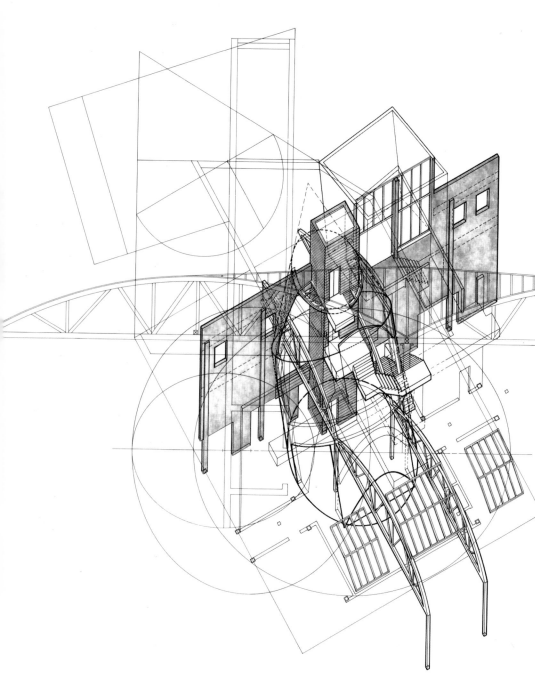

HAYDEN TRACT
3535 HAYDEN AVENUE

Inspection of an existing group of attached warehouse buildings reveals a 230 foot long shed, with pairs of parallel bowstring trusses supporting a vaulted roof.

Adjoining buildings are to be demolished as are the walls and roof enclosing the bowstrings. Only the parallel and attached bowstring pairs will remain.

Parking for 110 automobiles must fit on grade. No excavation, no decks: too expensive. But parking compresses the bowstrings from the south. So the bowstrings are to be cut to accommodate the cars (while one truss at the entrance is left intact).

Not yet completed the renovation is conceived as follows: the cut bowstring block locates the new structure consisting of three floors of office, conference, studio and warehousing. The cut ends support steel sun screens on the south wall. And the city-mandated street setback reveals an amended bowstring pair in elevation.

A steel frame (column tubes, wide flange beams) is positioned over the wooden trusses. An existing wooden post at the mid-point of a typical bowstring pair becomes the centre line of a two storey, clerestory lit circulation/exhibit space: a double-loaded interior street.

Street walls accommodate the hanging of a scatological collection of posters, album covers and assorted paraphernalia associated with the music business in Los Angeles.

The company self image: Berkeley of the 60s; the business reality: Reagan of the 80s.

A lobby divides the interior street into east and west sections. Behind the lobby is the main conference room. The lobby section is fossilised on the south exterior wall (parking/entry elevation). An executive conference room above and a canopy at the doors confirm the entrance.

This record company insists that the building will establish a recognisable company identity, assisting in the peddling of merchandise. Maybe they're right.

The hybrid interior elevation that results from the combination of old trusses and new steel frames suggests a needed revision in the conventional logic that often determines structure. The anomaly of the truss/steel frame is unlikely to occur in conventional construction. Perhaps it should.

99

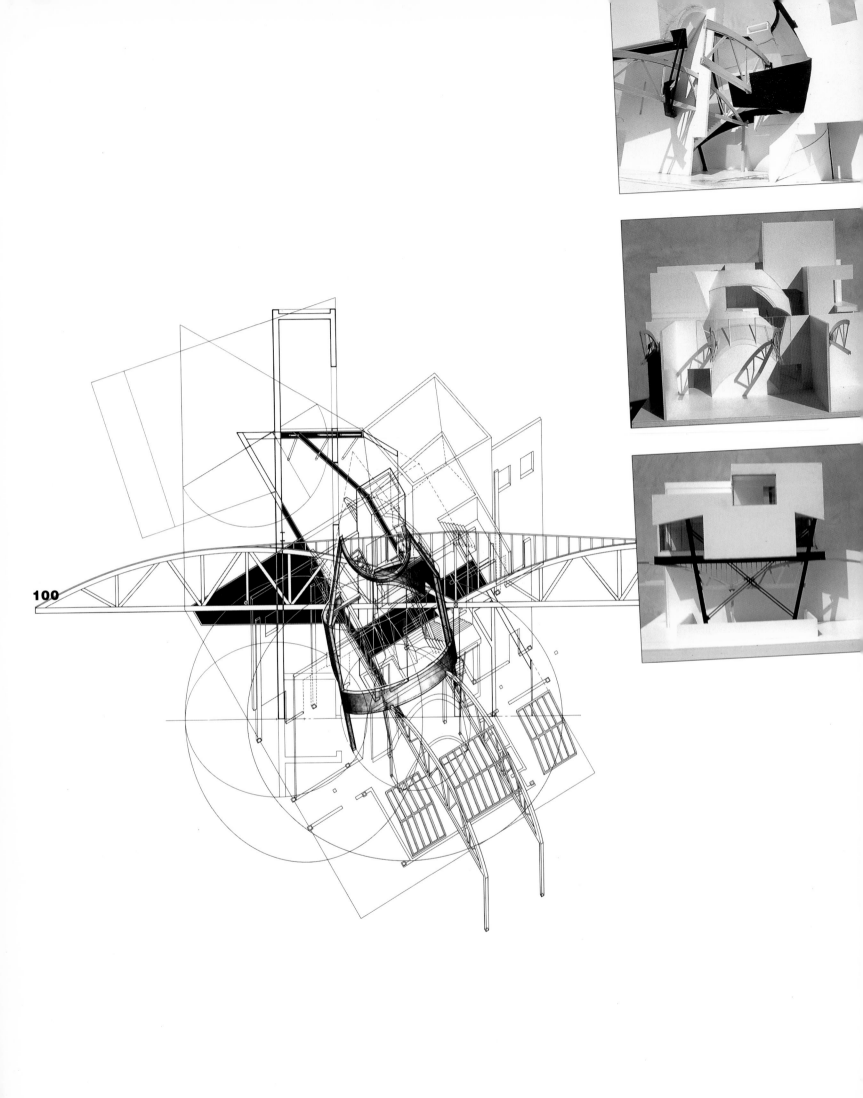

100

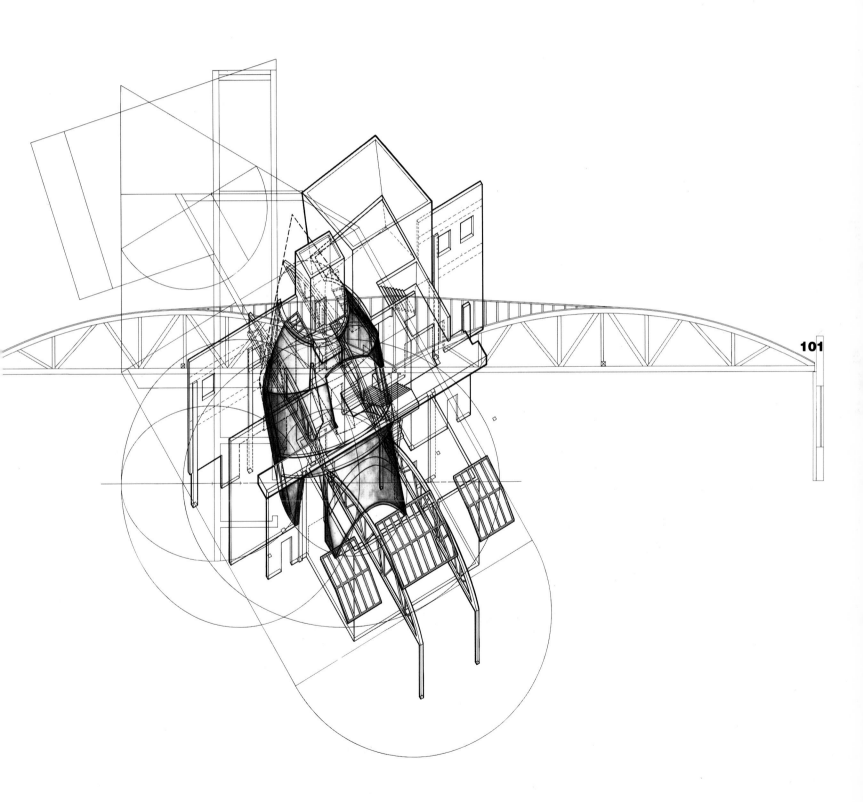

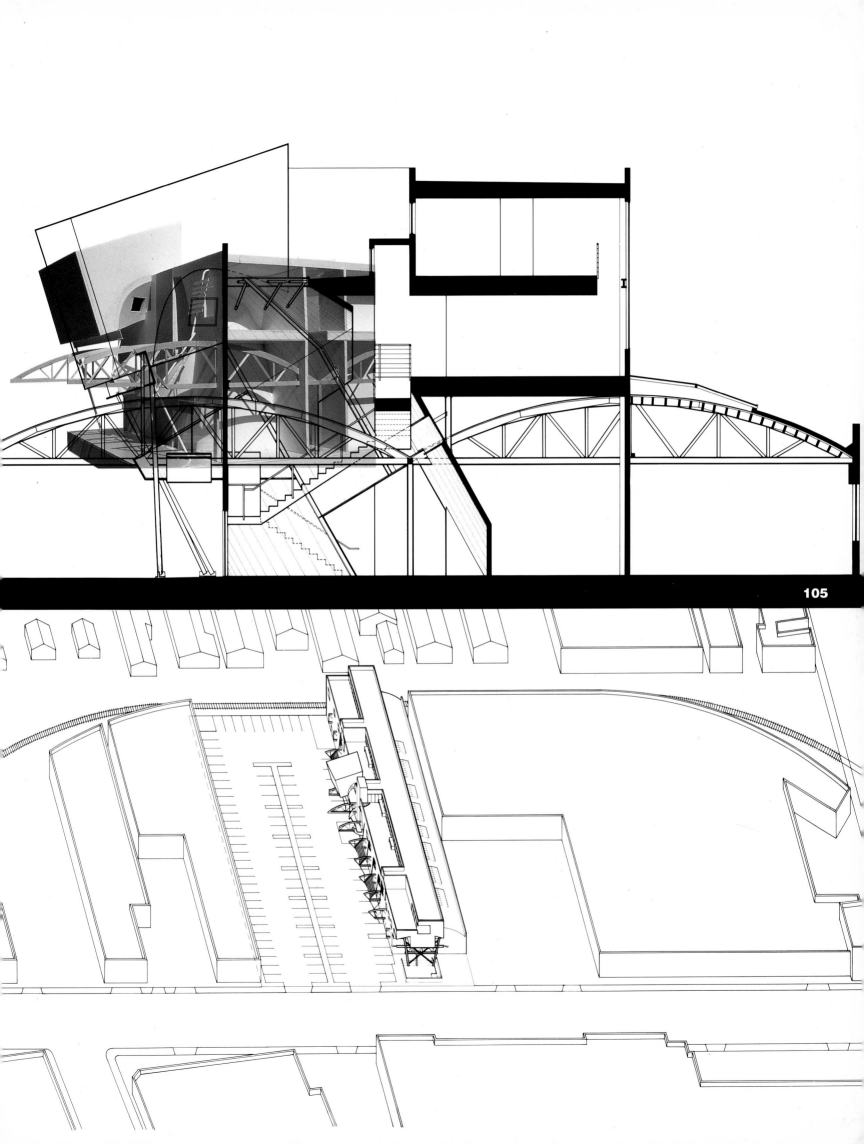

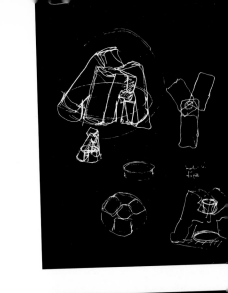

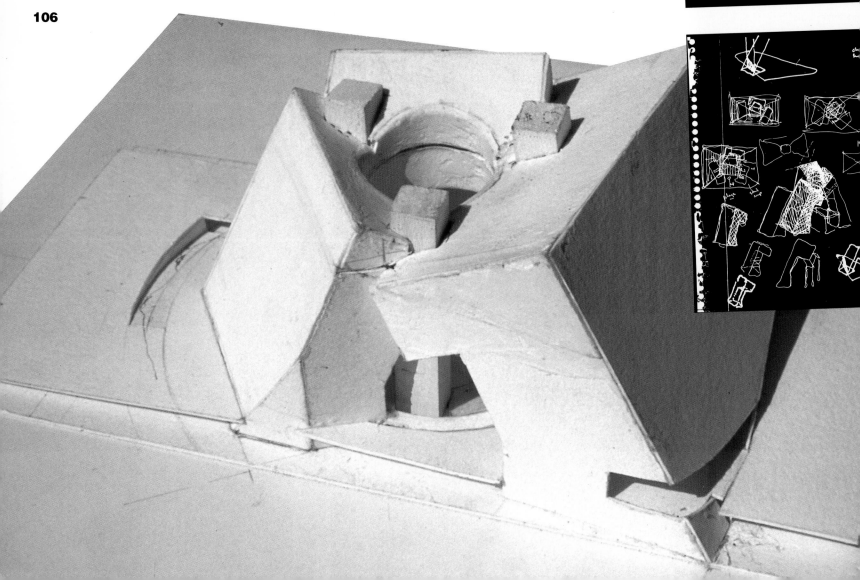

HAYDEN TRACT
WARNER AVENUE

Warner Avenue is part of the Hayden Tract site. Its scale, by intention, is colossal relative to its neighbours. Its essential role is planned as public and civic.

The building will be made from the intersection of three ten-storey 'hammers' which are to be surgically connected over a two-storey parking deck. The interior space created will serve as an enormous court for the performing arts. Surrounding the court will be civic facilities, offices and restaurants. The project adjoins the SPAR CITY right of way.

108

HAYDEN TRACT
HAYDEN TOWER

The project represents an important
planning step in the re-invention of the
decaying heavy-industrial area of Culver
City. Industrial tenants who occupied the
buildings on this and adjacent sites for the
last 30 years have gone out of business or
are now at work in Laredo, Taipei or Manila.
The project is not only an effort to give
impetus to a re-definition of a section of
West Los Angeles, but by implication is
representative of the need to revise
economic and land use patterns in many
deteriorating industrial portions of
American cities.

On the site, a 65 foot steel frame tower
once housed an enormous industrial press.
Adjoining the tower are two truss-supported
sheds originally used for warehousing and
manufacturing.

Once the tower's skin is removed leaving
only the frame, the sheds will be demolished, while the trusses are saved and
stock piled. It is envisaged that a new
single storey concrete block shed, princi-
pally for warehousing, will fill the site. The
roof of the new shed is to be a parking
deck; with holes cut in the deck providing
natural light to the ground floor.

The rest of the project is conceived as
follows: the old wood trusses supported on
steel columns are assembled around a
steel circulation cylinder, sliced through the
deck, which moves pedestrians from
parking to the main level warehouse space
or to adjoining offices and restaurant.

The trusses, radiating from the cylinder,
support a new pedestrian walkway, one
level above the deck, on which occupants
stroll to office and restaurant areas inside
the reconnoitred tower. A free-standing
conference building at this level provides a
private space where the owners can meet.

Stairs and elevator are attached to the
original steel frame. Trusses extend
through the original tower and a new,
enlarged tower volume is invented by
connecting points on the frame to the ends
of the radiating trusses. The extended
tower is wrapped with brass sheets. The
conference room is to be covered with
copper sheets.

The design strategy investigates use, re-
use and abuse of antecedents on the site.
The making of the project is like drawing on
a sheet of paper on which other drawings
exist. You erase and amend, but don't
entirely eradicate the previous presence.

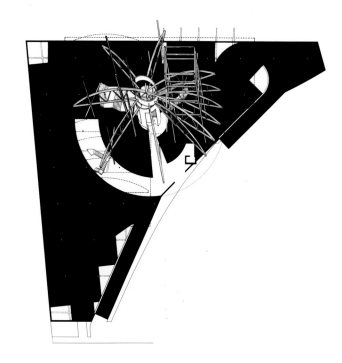

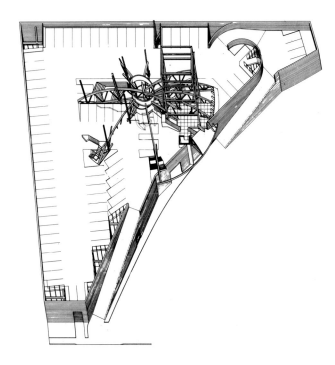

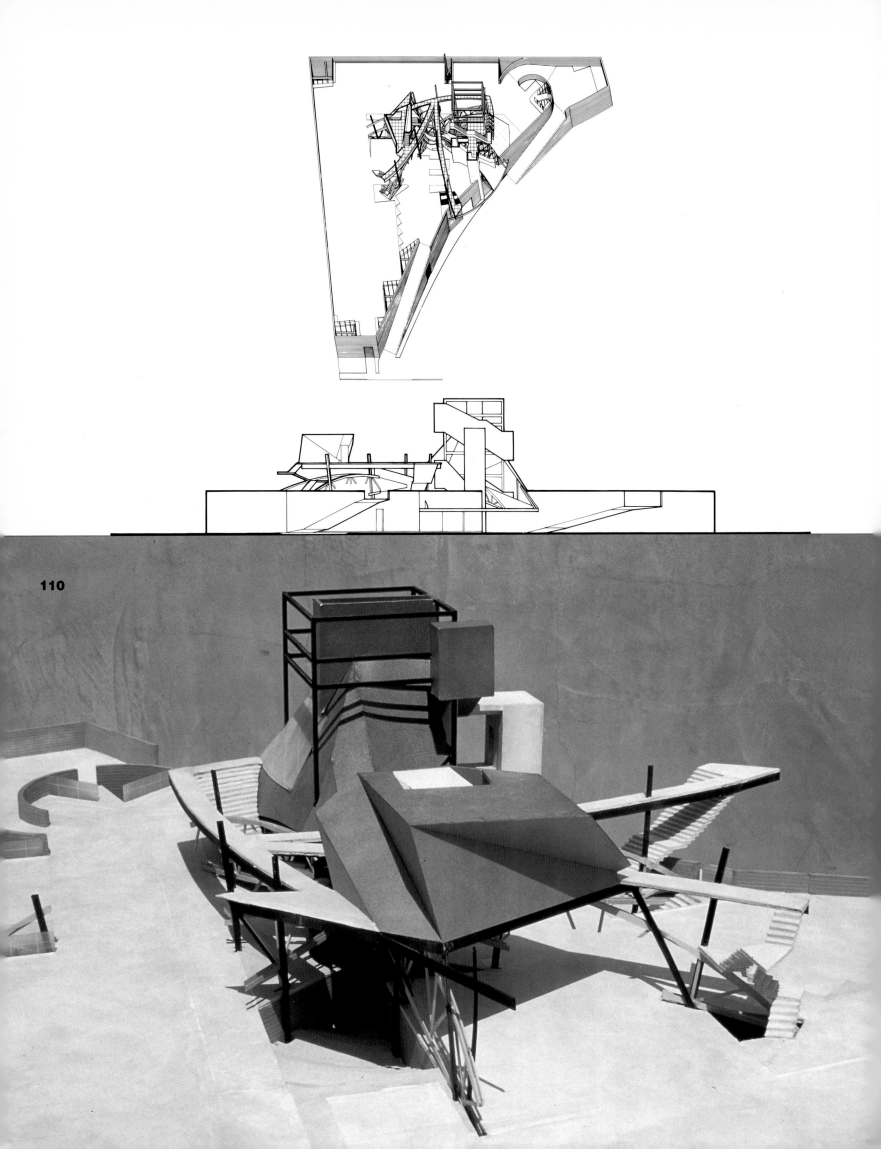

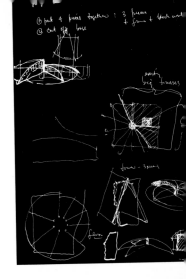

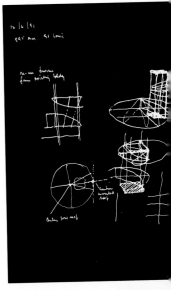

113

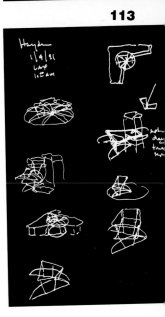

ABSTRACT

The removal of toxic waste from the site precipitated this project. An existing industrial warehouse building, three bays of bowstring trusses, currently sit on the site. Each bay is about 15,000 square feet. To facilitate the removal of the waste, the west bay was demolished. Two adjoining bays remain. A black masonry wall, 325 feet in length will seal the remaining bowstrings. Two floors of new office space will extend from the wall, supported on the wall and an exposed steel frame.

The conceptual design strategy comes from Heraclitus: you never step into the same form twice. The north end of the conceived project is three sided, the south end four sided. The section moves without warped plains between the three and four-sided figures. So both ends are recognisable, but the section between varies constantly. Mid-way is an open core with bathrooms, elevator, and stairs. Glazing follows a constant sill and head line in elevation, but varies as the section varies. A garden/theatre is proposed for an excavated portion of the site, with the bowstring area to be used as a proscenium stage.

114

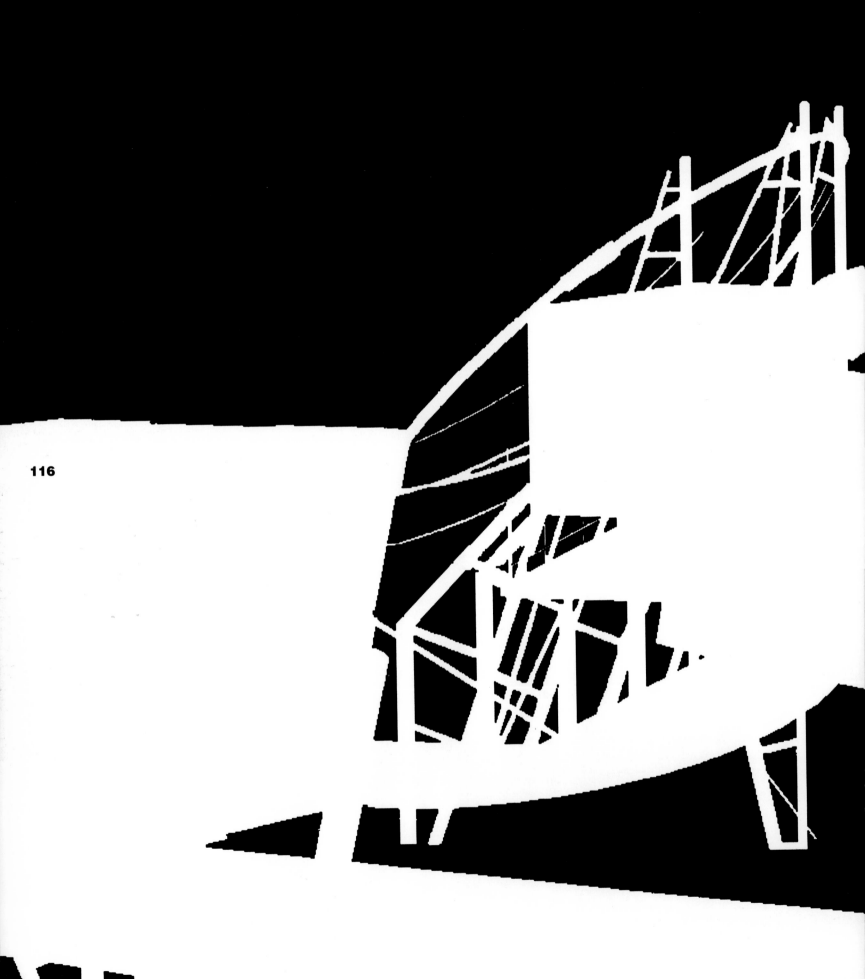

116

SPAR CITY
SOUTHERN PACIFIC AIR RIGHTS CITY

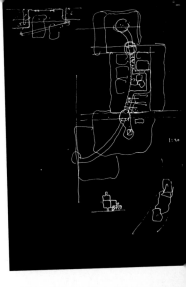

An abandoned Southern Pacific railroad right-of-way, about 50 feet in width, stretches approximately half a mile from the Los Angeles River to National Boulevard. The old tracks run through an area which for the past 50 years has been home to light industry and manufacturing. In the last ten years the industrial users have begun to relocate to areas where rent and labour costs are substantially less, for example: Japan, Korea and Mexico.

This area is perhaps a prototype for a number of dated industrial complexes, large and small, in the United States that must re-define or re-invent their urban purpose.

The route of SPAR CITY moves north-west through a district of warehouses, past an unbuilt site used as a city car park, and through an area of UCLA leased artist studios. Turning to the north, it adjoins a residential area of inexpensive apartments and modest single family homes, ending at National Boulevard, a major vehicular thoroughfare.

SPAR CITY's strategy is to re-define the area, increase its diversity, and reinforce and invigorate, where plausible, existing uses and activities. The project seeks both to begin again and to revive the existing context. These dual objectives are under-stood not as a conflict of intentions, but as mutually reinforcing goals.

The project developer controls the right-of-way and also owns many of the adjoining buildings. Parking will be provided in city-owned car parks, and shuttles (perhaps reusing the tracks) will deliver workers to their destinations along the route.

The design approach adopted for this project applies two metaphors; firstly the Chameleon, and secondly the cars of the freight train that once rolled through the area. The form of the project varies over its length as it extends, amends and reconfirms utilities that adjoin the right-of-way. These features will include: a major commercial gate at National Boulevard, multi-unit housing in the existing residential areas, shops, a theatre adjoining an existing restaurant, a street-bridge/office building (which metamorphosise as artist lofts and galleries), an amphitheatre, a hotel and parking, offices and warehouses. These diverse services demonstrate SPAR CITY's proposed development into an office/commercial/restaurant complex at the river.

The ground level will become a park and promenade, accessing the adjacent buildings along the right-of-way and the vertical circulation to air-rights buildings/bridges above.

Two characterisations exist for the buildings that adjoin the right-of-way: *friendly* and *unfriendly*. If a building is friendly and its owner/tenant selects to join the train, it opens to the right-of-way and the air-rights construction can abut or extend over the existing building. This suggests a series of new and re-constituted industrial structures along the line.

If the adjacency is unfriendly, SPAR CITY structures, and the new park, simply pass by. The original buildings continue to operate, as before, accessed from adja-cent streets. If adjacent properties are vacant the linear structure can extend perpendicular to itself, expropriating and exploring new territory.

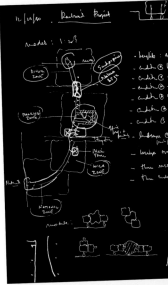

This plan is egalitarian and totalitarian. It adds to existing uses, it subtracts others, it entices, it compels but doesn't demand for its neighbours to join. It proposes to transform a debilitated area into a major civic component of the West Los Angeles area. Furthermore it will do this without public monies.

SPAR CITY is a conceptual and formal hypothesis. In the end it may appear in pieces, all together, or in an altered, and as yet undetermined, form. Received with great enthusiasm by the local City Council, it is an opportunity to reconstitute this portion of a dying, industrially based city.

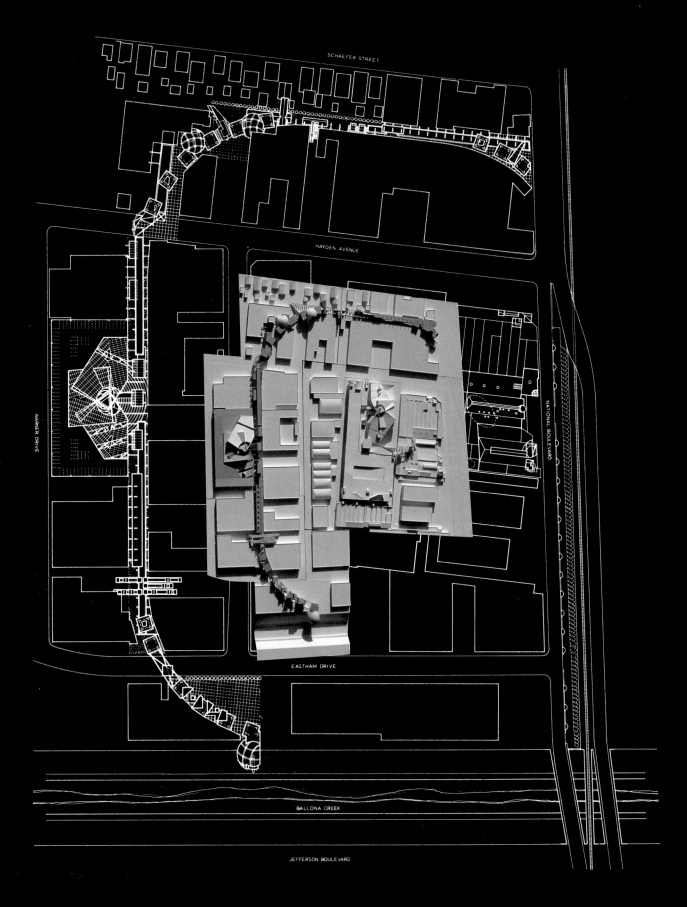

SCHAEFER STREET

HAYDEN AVENUE

WARNER DRIVE

NATIONAL BOULEVARD

EASTHAM DRIVE

BALLONA CREEK

JEFFERSON BOULEVARD

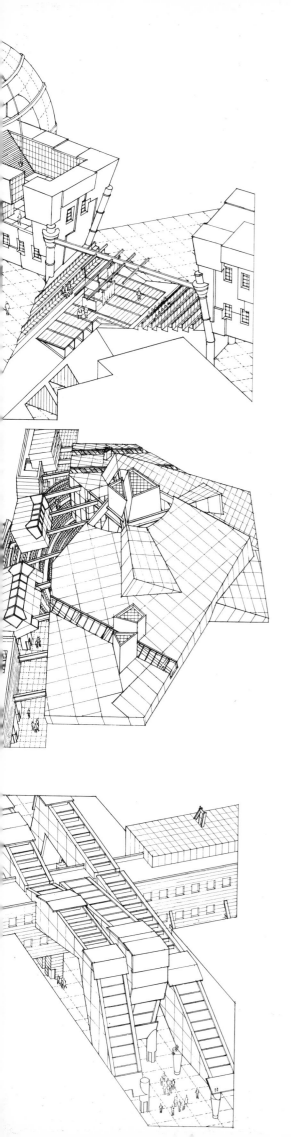

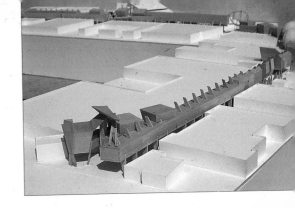

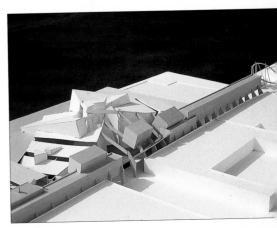

119

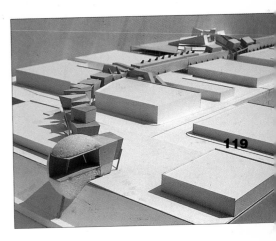

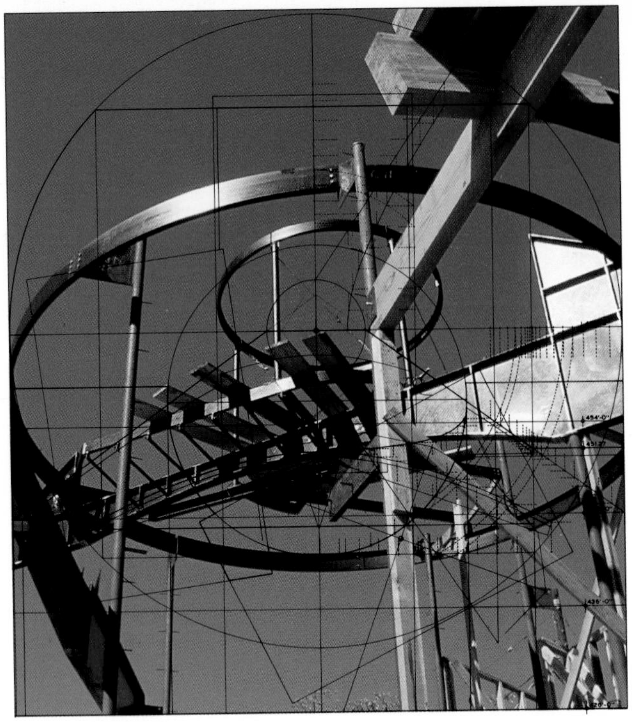

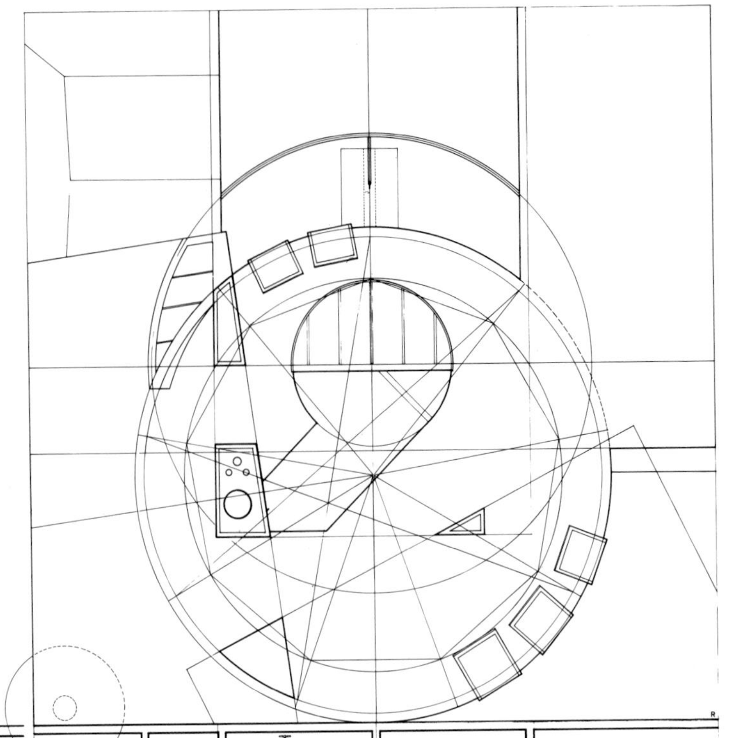

120

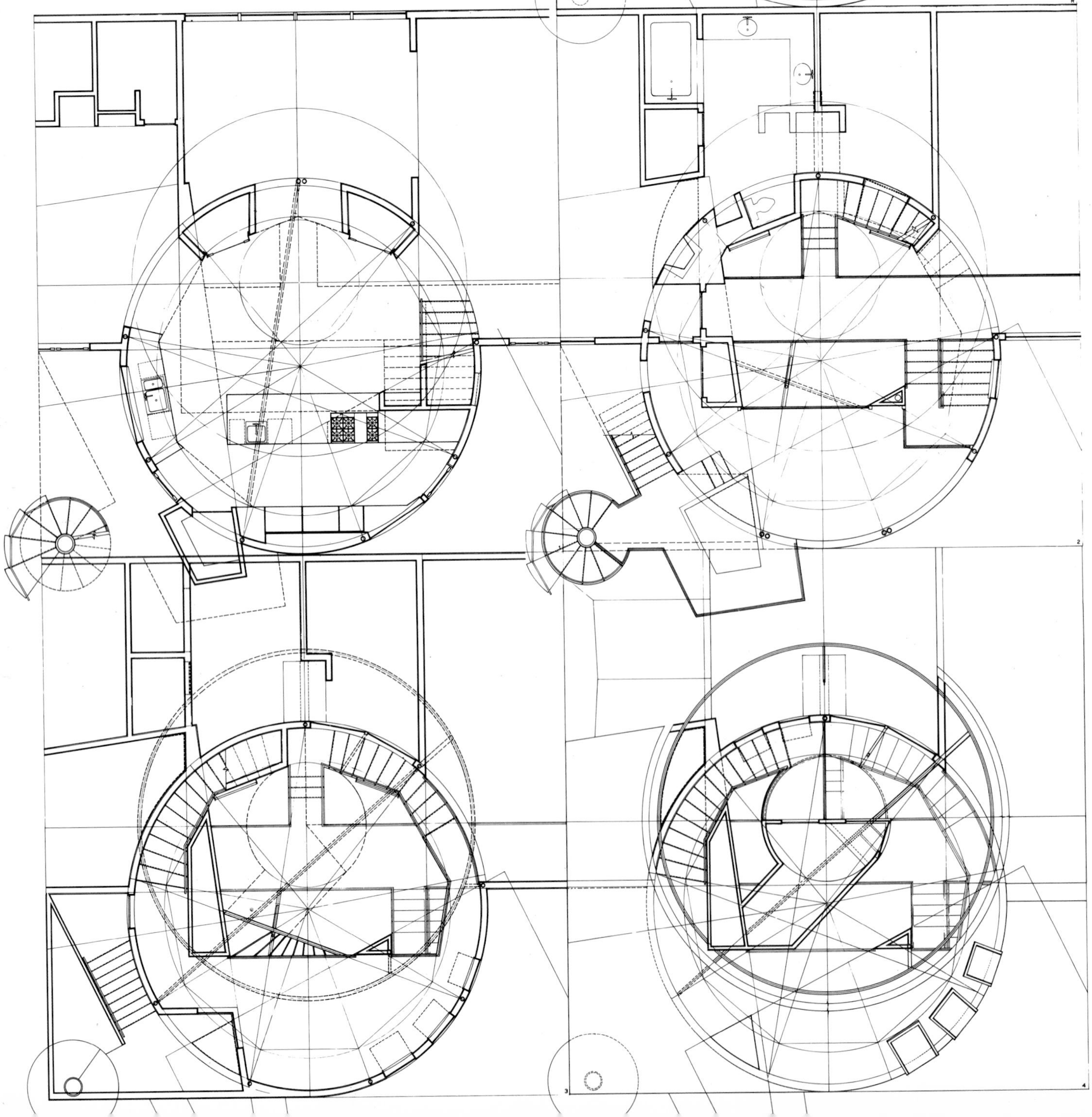

LAWSON/WESTEN HOUSE

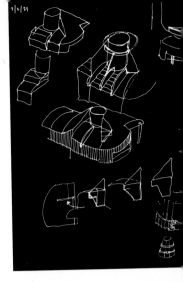

The clients should be acknowledged because both Tracy and Linda made a tremendous contribution to the realisation of this house. The kitchen is where they entertain, so that space became the focal element of the building and the leisure area. A cone becomes the roof shape of the cylindrical kitchen, but the centre of the cone is not the centre of the cylinder. The cone top is cut off to give the ocean view deck. The cone is sliced vertically, and that cut creates a curve, which is parabolic; this curve is then pulled towards the street, forming the vaulted roof. That is the idealised vault. The only literal instance is one rib which is fully extended at the entrance.

There's a mapping of the kitchen in plan, that sets a series of plan options, or rules. But as those rules are interpreted in the section, the connection between the hypothetical logic of the plan and the reality of the section seem to diminish. The sectional consequences don't necessarily correspond with the plan.

The geometric order, of the conical and cylindrical kitchen, depends primarily on the centre of a square, which is the geographic centre of the site. The centre of the square is also the centre of the cone. The apex of the vaulted roof is drawn through that centre point. A ring beam concentric to this centre supports the cone roof. The kitchen cylinder is adjusted to the south, tangent to one edge of the square. The cone and cylinder amend one another, creating a joint volume.

The original scheme for the building had three rectangular plan elements, the residue of which appears sporadically in the final kitchen section. Linda may come in and ask, 'Why is this piece of the kitchen over here?'. And the answer is, it's from the scheme that's not here any more. So there are obligations to a building that never was.

There's another section set up to determine the profile of the skylights above the vaulted roof. However, it was impossible to place the skylight in the most desirable place. The piece was continually adjusted in a vain attempt to prove that it was the profile that determined the position of the skylights, whereas in reality it was vice versa.

The front wall of the building is concrete. The rest of the building is one of those indefinable steel-trowelled plaster jobs. The window in the front wall is folded around a corner. In the original investigation, two walls and a floor were taken, and then a square was pushed into that corner, so that the square faced on to both walls and the floor. This was not the answer because the three faces no longer added up to a square. Furthermore, in the final rendition, the window did not meet the floor.

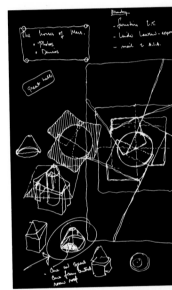

This may be perceived as an inclination towards conceptual dissection, towards taking apart buildings at both a large scale, (meaning walls and roofs), and the next scale down (doors and windows) and further still (to screws and washers). It is, but there is also a way to re-assemble the pieces, both apart and together.

121

Owners: Linda Lawson and Tracy Westen
Interior Design Consultant: Tracy Sonka Stultz, ASID
Structural Engineer: Gary Davis, Davis Design Group/Davis-Fejes Design
Mechanical Engineer: Greg Tchamitchian, AEC Systems
Lighting Consultant: Saul Goldin, Saul Goldin and Associates
Furniture/Fixture Fabrication: Tom Farrage, Farrage & Co
General Contractor: John Blackley, Admiral Construction

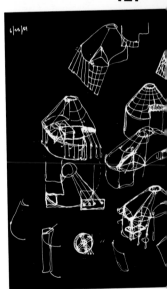

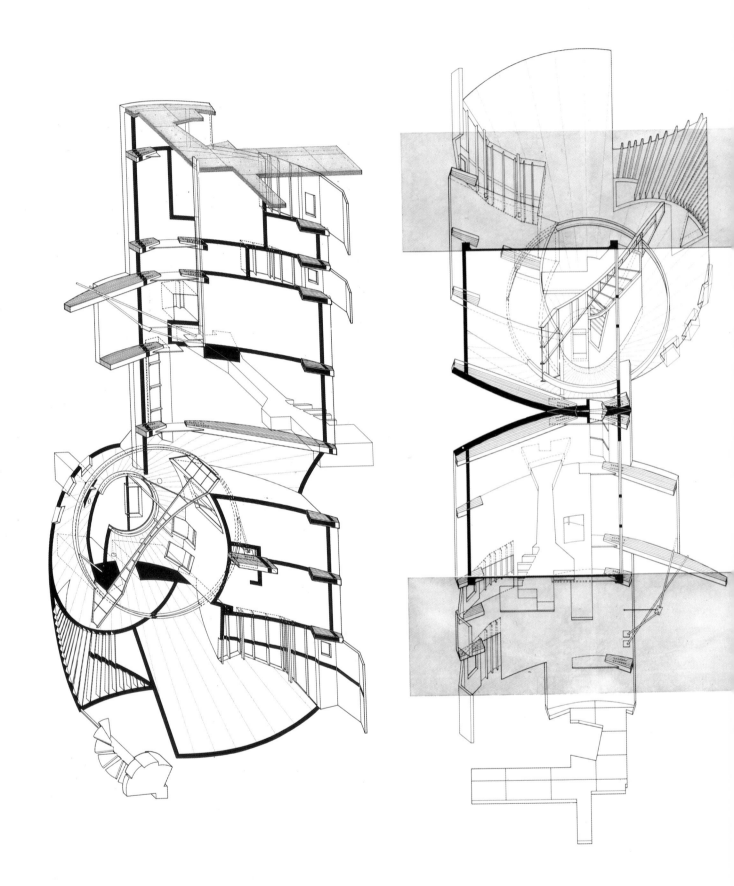

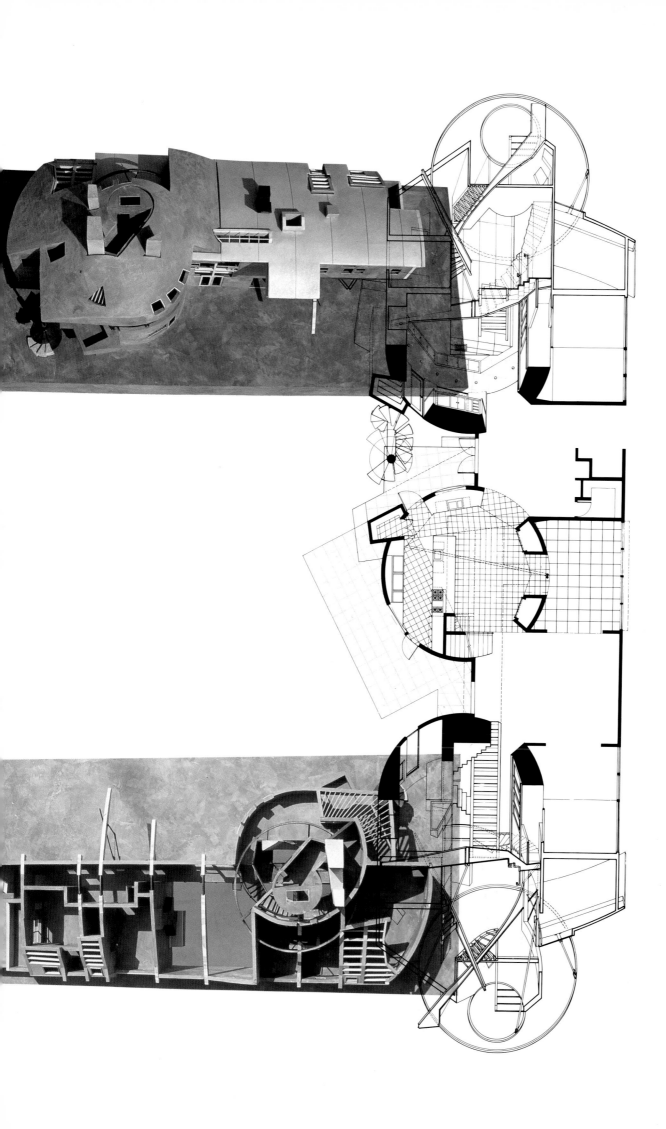
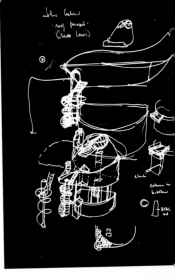

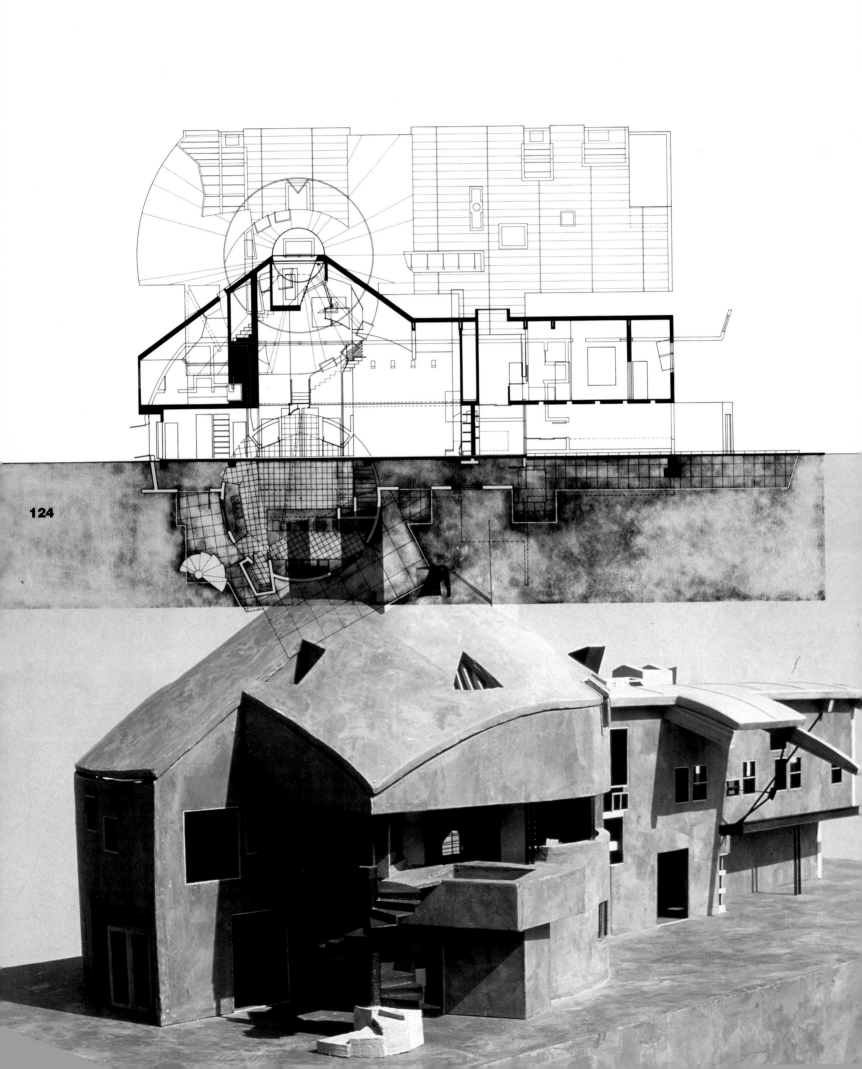

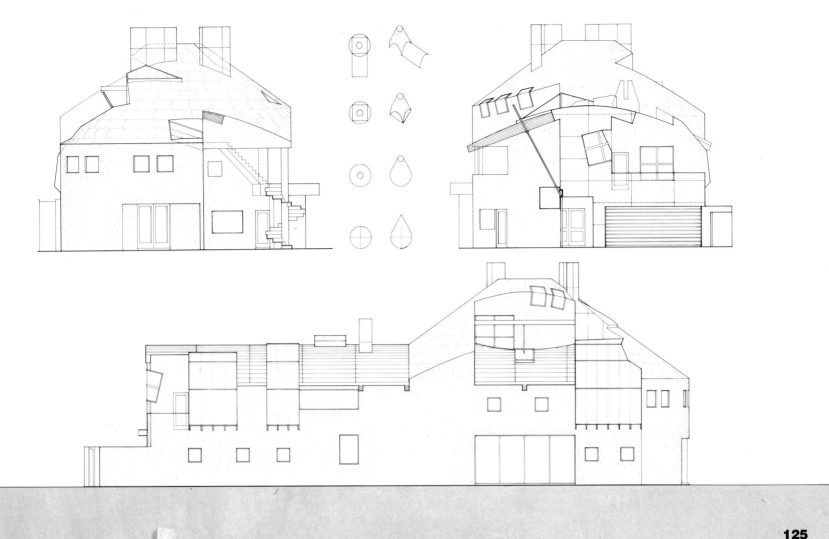

126

FURNITURE

The model for furniture is the ubiquitous machine – a hybrid view of the machine as omnipresent, not as an idol or an ideal, but with conflicting aspects both positive and negative.

There's also a hedonism here (love of joinery, love of assembly, love of the artifact) not in a repetitive, 'off the shelf' way, but more introverted and personal.

Collaboration in all cases is with Tom Farrage and Company.

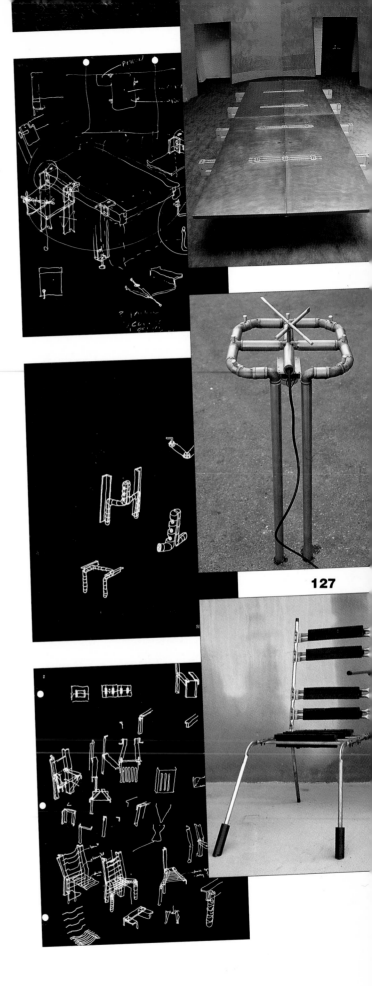

SAMITAUR
I & II

Samitaur, parts I & II, is an office building built over a road in the south-western section of Los Angeles. The area is a mixture of one and two-storey industrial and manufacturing buildings constructed in the 50s and 60s, interconnected by a network of public and private roads.

The project site is a privately owned road terminated by a complex of one-storey, saw-tooth roofed buildings that house offices, storage and food preparation facilities. Existing single-storey buildings on either side of the road contain light manu-facturing. The new office block will be lifted on circular steel columns, allowing trucks and cars continued access to the facilities on the same level. It will provide expanded office space and will be linked by elevator and stairs to production facilities in the old shed at grade level.

The redevelopment is envisaged in the following manner: columns supporting the office block are positioned to avoid loading doors adjacent to the access road. Diago-nal bracing at street level and five rigid frames address lateral problems. Tapered steel beams span between the columns. The new first floor is lifted above existing one-storey roofs allowing natural light into the covered street from east and west. In time it is anticipated that the industrial tenants will be replaced by commercial tenants and the road will become a com-mercial walking street.

A height limit of 48 feet confines the office to two floors over required truck clear-ances. Fire regulations limit the building width to the width of the private road. The roof access is for service only, although it is likely to become the locale for informal office gatherings offering unrestricted views in all directions.

Three circumstantial conditions require exceptions to the essential office block: firstly, positioned to address approaching traffic at the street entry, a modified conical section is carved from the orthogonal block, providing exterior deck space and an open

stair to the street. Secondly, on the west face of the office block is a five-sided, two storey courtyard, planted with grass, irrigated from the beam network above. The modified pentagon is located above a secondary vehicle access point. Thirdly, at the north end of the building, adjoining the elevator-stair core, the building block slides over the saw-tooth shed below, supported again on steel columns which penetrate the existing building. Fire codes require a raised first floor height to clear the roof below. The resulting one-and-a-half storey space is the corporate board room.

To summarise: truck clearance below, and zoned height and width limits above, define the essential building block. Column locations are determined by the position of loading dock doors along the road. Beams follow the columns. Truss joisted floors follow the beams. Two office floors are stacked. An elevator connects old to new. At two essential access points the block organisation is countered, and at a third location, no longer over the road, a modi-fied floor height generates the board room.

Owner: Frederick Norton Smith
Structural Engineer: Joe Kurily, Kurily Szymandski Tchirkow
Mechanical Engineer: Paul Antieri, I & N Consulting Engineers
Electrical Engineer: Paul Immerman, I & N Consulting Engineers
Lighting Consultant: Saul Goldin, Saul Goldin and Associates
Construction Manager/General Contractor: Southgate Construction

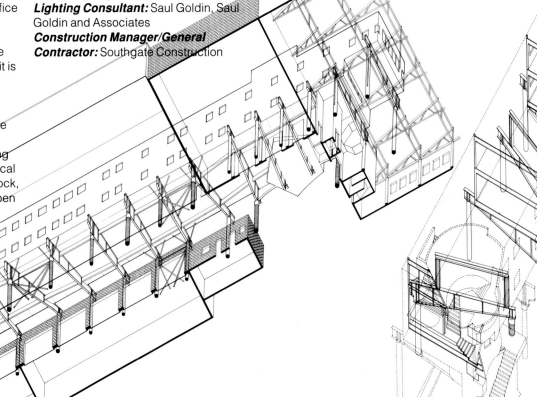

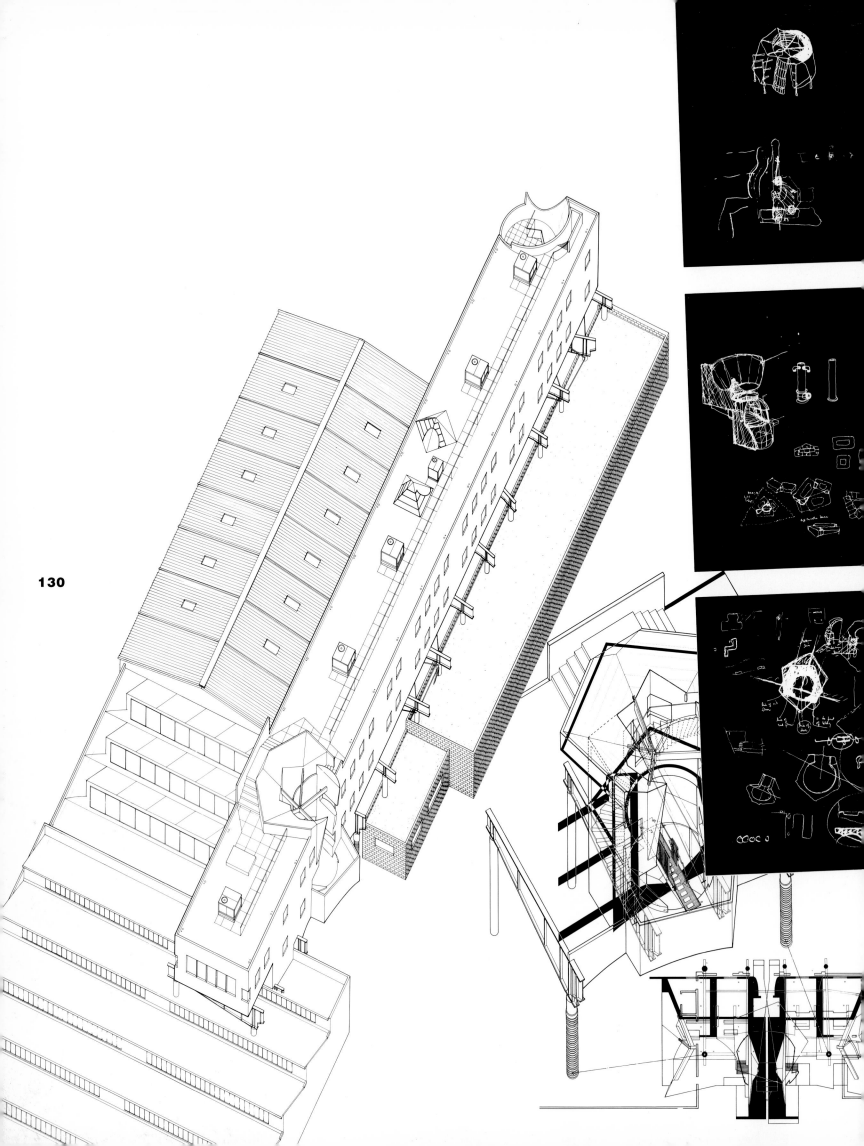

130

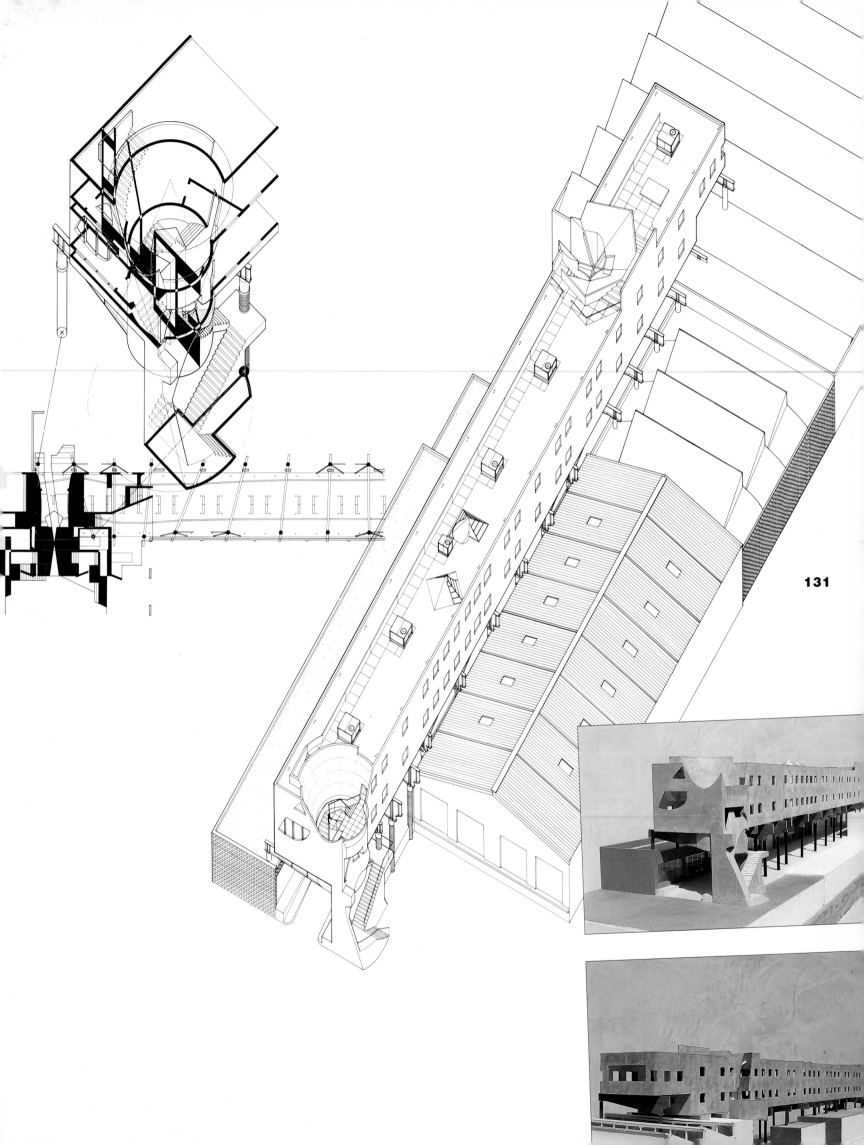

131

SAMITAUR
III, THE HOOK

Phase III of Samitaur, The Hook, was
designed about the same time as the
Goalen project, though not yet completed,
and the two are strategically related.

In plan there is an inter-penetration of a
circle and a six-sided figure. The intention
on the site is to offer an enclosure, an
introverted public space as a counter to the
linear, extroverted building of phase I and II.

The Hook will terminate in an almost
block-like form which follows the plan
profile of a major street to the north.

The primary entrance is at the conjunction of phase II and III, the pentagonal
court, pool and stair. Secondarily one will
enter through the block.

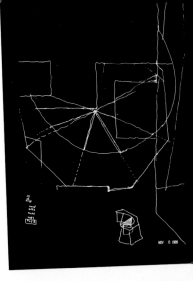

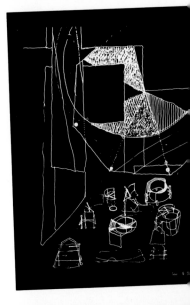

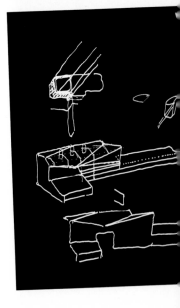

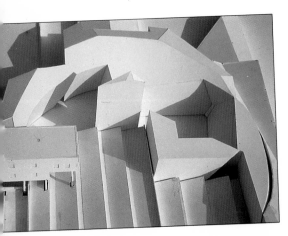

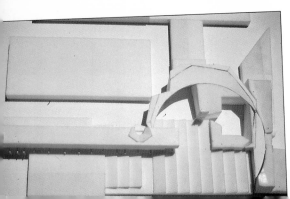

SAMITAUR
IV, THE SQUID

The fourth piece of Samitaur is envisaged as free standing. It is to be the link between the Box to the west and Samitaur I, II, III to the east.

The building section moves between two knowns: one four-sided, the other elliptical. The section evolves perpetually. So the building is never a single shape but always varying parts of two.

A portion of the roof is lifted away, creating two interior courts. An earthquake fault line runs through the corner of the site, terminating the building on the south edge.

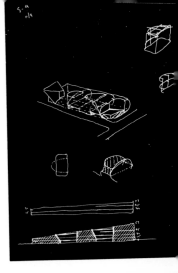

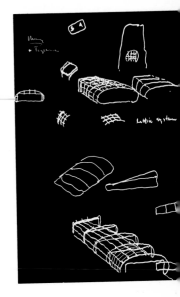

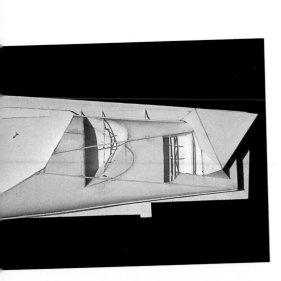

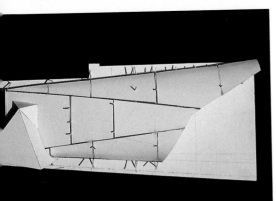

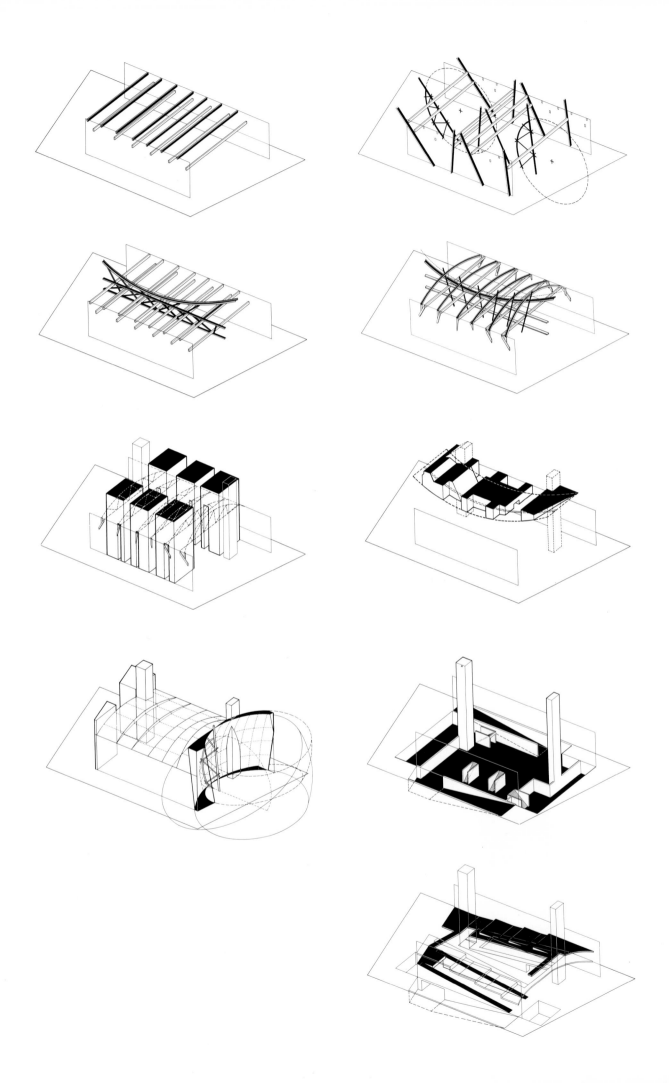

134

IBIZA PASEO

The last piece of unbuilt commercial property borders the port and waterfront on the Spanish Island of Ibiza. Across the port to the south is Dalt Vila, the old walled city that traces its history from Punic times: Carthaginians and Romans to Arabs, Castilians and Catalans. Ship followed ship, conqueror followed conqueror over the years, over the Mediterranean to Ibiza. So ship motifs: hull, oar and sail, merge in the final building form. The supplanting of one conqueror's idols with another's is reiterated in the building; as an aggregate of pieces in, on, around and over one another, much like the aggregate construction of diverse forms over millennia in Dalt Vila.

The building was designed a step at a time, with each step as an amendment to the previous step and a forecast of what might follow. Each progression contains aspects of space, form, structure, material, site circumstance and programme. But no stage is entirely any or all of these. The design conclusion may appear to be the consequence of a logical sequence of thinking, but only in retrospect.

Operationally the predicted building is first a street (a paseo), open on the ends and enclosed along the top and sides. Its first responsibility is to the public: pedestrian circulation along the voluminous paseo, edged by retail and restaurants, re-connecting the waterfront promenade to a parallel commercial street behind.

Bordering the visualised paseo is a pair of interlocking ramps entered from opposite ends on each street. The ramps move pedestrians past shops that sit on platforms raised on the two ramps. Bridges connect the ramps across the paseo. The top two levels (six repetitive blocks) contain private office space, accessed by ramp or elevator. Walks and decks at both office levels offer exercise areas and views of the Port, the Mediterranean and the old city.

The long sides of the building (east and west) are set back four metres from the property lines. They face new apartment and retail blocks similar in height and width. Through the glass the progression of ramps, and the organisational framework of structure, glazing and the office blocks, is legible. The port elevation, a selected accretion of building elements (sphere, block, ramp), mixes public, glass-enclosed decks with offices, restaurants and bars, thereby offering an opportunity to study the old city from the new.

The project aspires to suggest a sensibility conscious of tradition that simultaneously enjoys its stretching and remodelling.

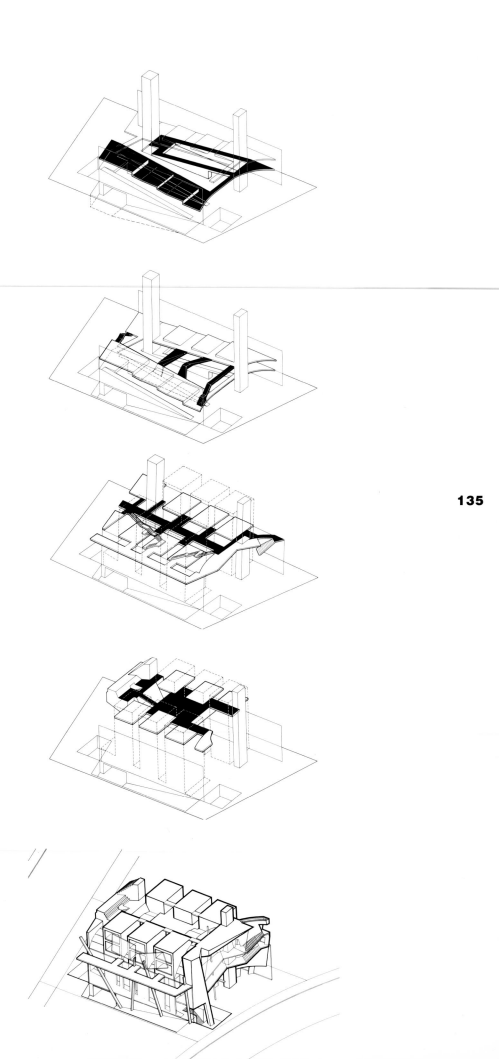

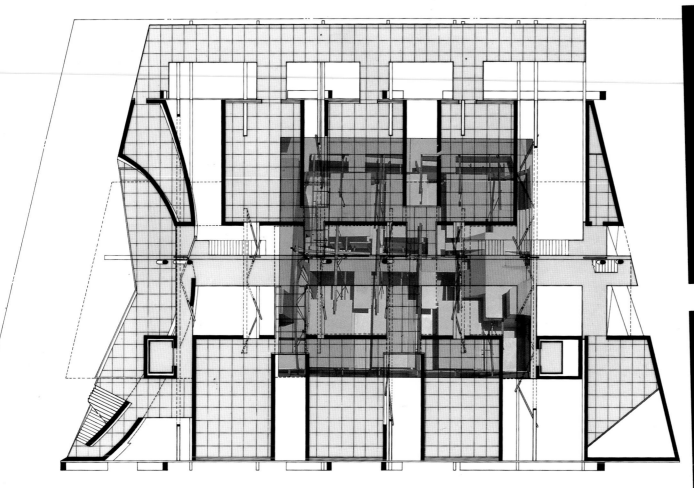

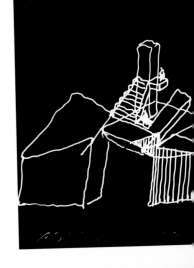

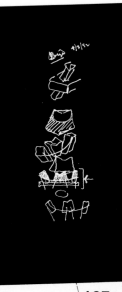

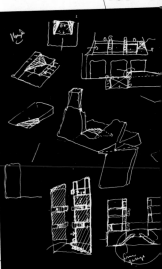

138

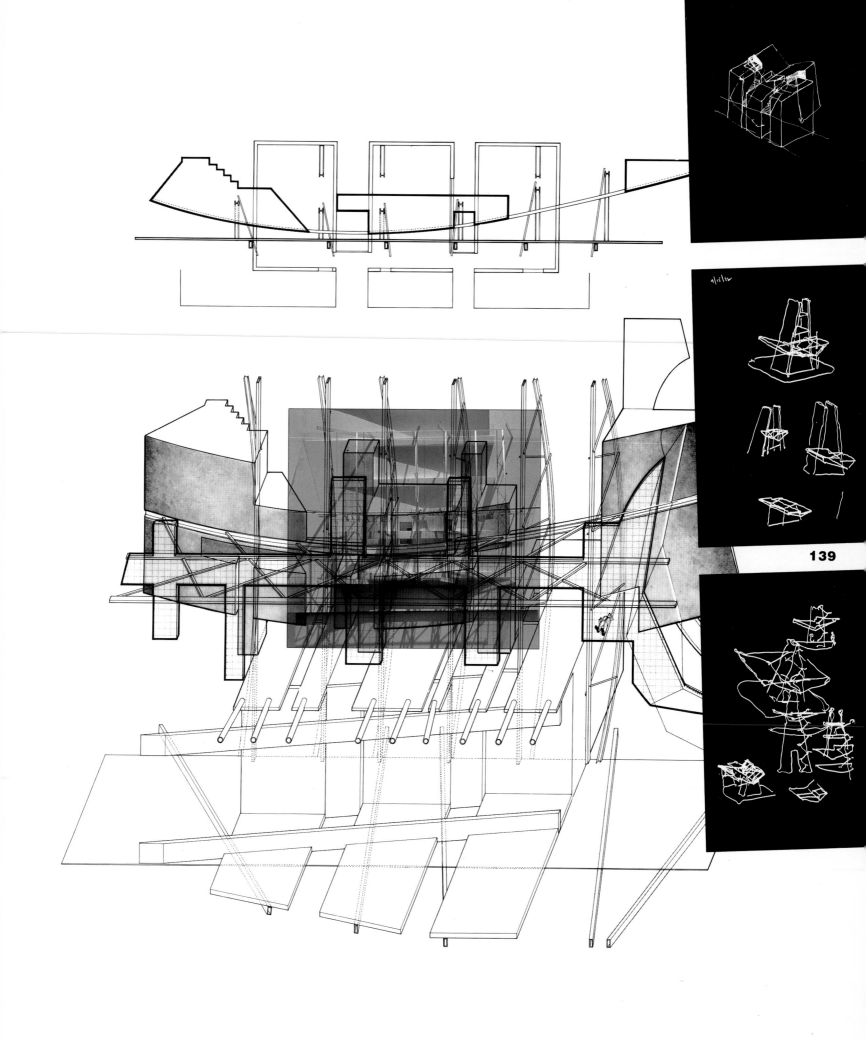

ARONOFF

P & D own a nondescript tract house on the northern side of the Santa Monica Mountains. The property stretches north-west of the existing house and down a slope to the Santa Monica Conservancy, a beautiful wooded area extending for several miles, protected in perpetuity from development.

The new guest house is a pleasurable toy for its owners, their employees, guests and children. The building can be climbed on, examined, and used as a viewing platform. The building location and the configuration of floors and windows make full advantage of the spectacular views of the forest.

The project is positioned at the transition from the flat to the sloping portion of the site. Furthermore it is adjacent to the south-west property line, thereby exploiting the vista without interrupting the existing house's view. The position of the new house also allows clear visibility and access from the street for those who come to it directly to do business.

The project contains three floors: the top level studio/executive offices for the owners; an office floor at grade for a business with three employees and a separate apartment below for an elderly father. The roof, designed as a stepped bleacher/deck with open and covered areas, is oriented to the view of the Conservancy area and the San Fernando Valley. It is accessible from all levels via a stair that runs along the perimeter of the house. It is also accessible internally, directly from the third floor.

The middle level is the office floor for three employees, used in conjunction with owners' offices on the top floor. The apartment at the lowest level has elevator access, a covered deck area and an open patio. All levels may be accessed from the middle level lobby or from the exterior.

Rather than stacking floors as a building steps to acknowledge a hillside profile, the guest house emerges from a conical cut dug at the edge of the hill. The project, secured at the edge, combines sphere and cube, neither quite legible.

So . . . placed precariously at the top of a slope; stabilised by the conical cut; a threat to roll as a sphere; re-anchored by the cube, the guest house is a stable instability.

Owners: Pamela and Richard Aronoff
Structural Engineer: Robert Lawson, Robert Lawson Structural Engineers
Mechanical Engineer: Greg Tchamitchian, AEC Systems
Steel Model Fabrication: Tom Farrage, Farrage & Co

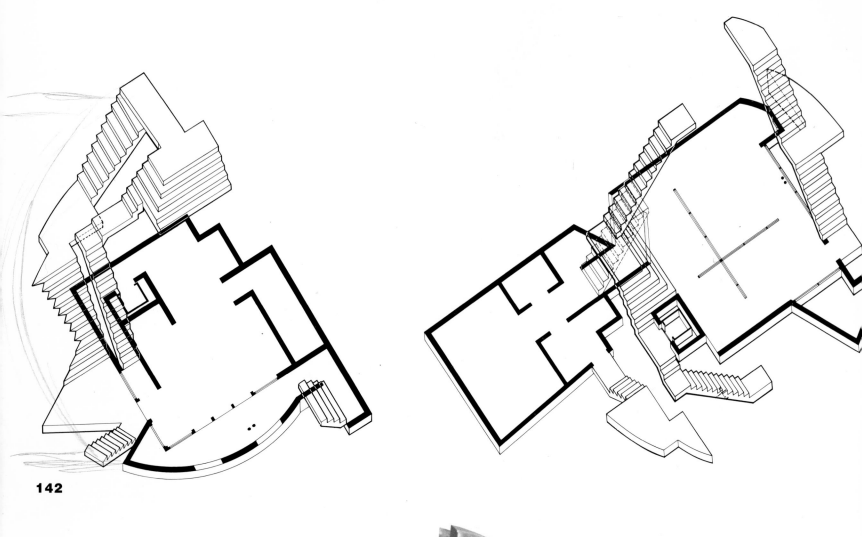

142

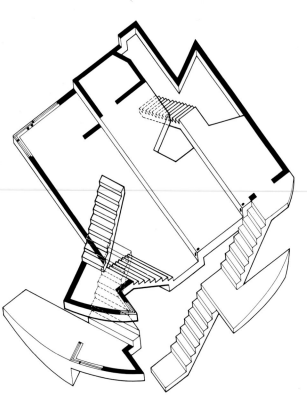

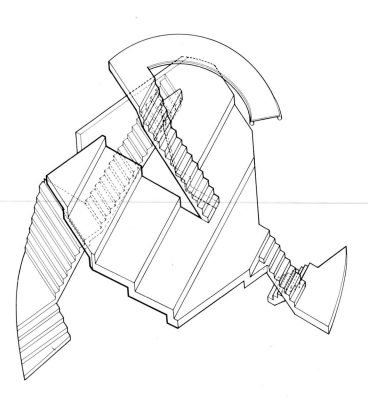

143

SELECTED EXHIBITS/ CATALOGUES

- Aspen Art Museum, Current work, Aspen, Colorado, June 3 – July 4, 1993.
- Harvard University, Graduate School of Design, Current work, Cambridge, Massachusetts, Spring 1993.
- Santa Monica Museum of Art, 'Angels & Franciscans: Innovative Architecture from Los Angeles and San Francisco', February 7 – March 1993.
- Progressive Architecture 'New Public Realm', solutions from the competition, touring exhibition; Washington, DC; New York; Toronto; Denver; San Francisco; Los Angeles; October 23 – March 20, 1992. Catalogue.
- University of California, Los Angeles, Graduate School of Architecture, 'Excavation', Los Angeles, California, October 19 – November 6, 1992.
- University of Zagreb, 'Houses in Los Angeles, California', Zagreb, Croatia, Fall 1992. Catalogue.
- GA Gallery, 'Contemporary Architectural Freehand Drawing', curated by Yukio Futagawa, Toyko, Japan, September 12 – October 18, 1992.
- 65 Thompson Street, Gagosian/Castelli Gallery, 'Angels and Franciscans: Innovative Architecture from Los Angeles and San Francisco', curated by Susan de Menil and Bill Lacy, New York, September 26 – November 7, 1992. Catalogue.
- Architectural Design Symposium/Exhibition, 'Theory and Experimentation' presented by Andreas Papadakis, London, England, June 9 – June 23, 1992. Catalogue.
- Gallery of Functional Art, 'Architects' Art 1992', curated by Lois Lambert, Santa Monica, California, February 1992.
- Bartlett School of Architecture and Urban Design, London, Great Britain November 1991.
- Osterreichisches Museum für Angewandte Kunst, Vienna, Austria, curated by Peter Noever, July 1991. Catalogue.
- Venice Art Walk, Venice, California, June 12, 1991.
- Los Angeles Contemporary Exhibitions, 11th Annual Benefit Art Auction, Los Angeles, California, October 1990.
- Salle des Tirages du Credit Foncier de France, curated by Oliver Boissiere and Les Editions du Demi-Cercle, Paris, France, June 27 – July 13, 1990.
- Harvard Graduate School of Design, 'Midnight at the Oasis', March 15 – April 14, 1990.
- Museum of Contemporary Art, 'Blueprints for Modern Living: History and Legacy of the Case Study Houses', Los Angeles, California,

October 14, 1989 – February 18, 1990. Catalogue.
- World Biennial of Architecture, 'Interarch 89' Exhibit, Sofia, Bulgaria, June 20 – June 26, 1989.
- Gallery of Functional Art, 'Architects' Art' Exhibit, Santa Monica, California, January 3 – March 3, 1989.
- Los Angeles/AIA Award Winners Exhibition, J Paul Getty Museum, Malibu, California, September 1988.
- Neo-Con, Lamp for Formica Corp, Chicago, Illinois, June 1988.
- National AIA Award Winners Exhibition, New York, May 1988.
- The Architectural League of New York, Exhibit: Experimental Tradition: Twenty-five years of American Architectural Competitions, Escondido Competition Drawings, New York, May – June 1988. Catalogue.
- GA Gallery, 'The Emerging Generation in USA', Tokyo, Japan, October 1987. Catalogue.
- The Architectural League of New York, 'Emerging Voices', New York, September 1986. Catalogue.
- Harvard Graduate School of Design, 'The Making of Architecture – The Indigent As King', Cambridge, Massachusetts, April 9 – 23, 1985. Catalogue.
- GA Gallery, 'California Architecture: Eric Moss/Morphosis', Tokyo, Japan, April – June, 1985. Catalogue.
- The Architectural Association, 'Los Angeles Now', London, England, April 2 – May 21, 1983. Catalogue.
- La Jolla Museum of Modern Art, 'The California Condition – A Pregnant Architecture', November 13, 1982 – January 2, 1983. Catalogue.
- 'Paris Biennial', Paris, France, August 1982. Catalogue.

AWARDS

- AIA/Los Angeles Design Award, Nara Convention Center, November 1992
- National AIA Interior Design Award, Gary Group, June 1992
- National AIA Interior Design Award, 8522 National Building, June 1992
- Progressive Architecture Design Award, P & D Guest House, January 1992
- Progressive Architecture Design Award, Samitaur Offices, January 1992
- California Council AIA Urban Design Award, 8522 National Complex, November 1991

- AIA/Los Angeles Design Award, Gary Group, October 1991
- AIA/Los Angeles Design Award, SMA, October 1991
- Interiors Award: Best Design in Adaptive Re-Use, Qualitative Research Centre, January 1991
- AIA/Los Angeles Design Award, Paramount Laundry Building, October 1990
- Metropolitan Home Design 100 Editorial Award, Eric Owen Moss, April 1990
- National AIA Honor Award, Central Housing Office Building, May 1989
- AIA/Los Angeles Design Award, 8522 National Building, October 1988
- National AIA Honor Award, 8522 National Building, May 1988
- California Council AIA Merit Award, 8522 National Building, April 1988
- California Council AIA Merit Award, The Petal House, March 1986
- Architectural Record Award Winning Interiors, World Savings and Loan, September 1984
- AIA/Los Angeles Design Award, The Fun House, November 1983
- AIA/Los Angeles Design Award, The Petal House, October 1983
- AIA/Sunset Magazine Western Home Awards, The Petal House, September 1983
- California Council AIA Merit Award, Morgenstern Warehouse, March 1981
- AIA/Los Angeles Design Award, Morgenstern Warehouse, November 1979
- Progressive Architecture Design Award, Morgenstern Warehouse, November 1978
- AIA/Sunset Magazine Western Home Awards, Playa del Rey Duplex, September 1977

PHOTOGRAPHIC CREDITS

Tom Bonner, pp8, 40-42, 44-49, 66, 82, 83; Donatella Brun, pp30, 36; Todd Conversano, front cover, pp17-23, 37, 50-54, 56, 58-9, 85 Right, 86, 91, 94-97, 100, 102-108, 110, 111-115, 118-120, 123, 124-127, 129, 131, 132, 133, 136-143; Peter Cook, pp62, 63, 80 Left; Sheng-Yuan Hwang, p26: Frank Jackson, 81 Right, 84, 87; Joe Lynch, p60; Grant Mudford, pp70, 72, 77, 78, 79, 80 Right, 81 Centre; Ron Pollard, pp26, 28, 32, 33; J Scott Smith, pp24, 34, 38; Tim Street-Porter, pp64, 65, 67-69; Alex Vertikoff, pp6, 88-90, 92, 127 Above Left.

144